A Pictorial History of the
WORLD WAR II YEARS

A PICTORIAL HISTORY OF

THE

WORLD

WAR II

YEARS

EDWARD JABLONSKI

Maps by Rafael Palacios

DOUBLEDAY & COMPANY, Inc.
Garden City, New York

The Airborne Symphony: Copyright © 1946 by Chappell
& Co., Inc. Copyright Renewed by the Estate of Marc
Blitzstein. Publication and allied rights controlled by
Chappell & Co., Inc. International Copyright Secured.
ALL RIGHTS RESERVED. Used by permission.

LIBRARY OF CONGRESS CATALOG CARD NUMBER 77-73328

Library of Congress Cataloging in Publication Data

Jablonski, Edward.
A pictorial history of the World War II years.

Includes index.
1. World War, 1939-1945—Campaigns.　I.　Title.
D743.J28　　　　940.53　　　　77-73328
ISBN 0-385-12350-7

9　8　7　6　5　4

For H.K.

*It is difficult to remember that events
now far in the past were once in the future.*

—Frederic W. Maitland

Contents

AUTHOR'S NOTE

THE BULK of the picture research for this volume (about 99.9%) is the work of Barbara Gilson of Nelson Doubleday, Inc. We are both grateful also for the assistance of Paul White of the National Archives. We thank other sources for photographs, among them the United States Air Force; the Imperial War Museum, London; Ordnance Museum, U.S. Army, Aberdeen, Maryland; and my son, David, who supplied a number of little known photos of the war in North Africa; and to Robert Jackson of Culver Pictures.

E. J.

A Pictorial History of the
WORLD WAR II YEARS

Prelude

Historians do not agree upon the opening date of World War II. Depending on the point of view, the political inclination, the ax to grind, or some newly discovered secret paper, any one of several would do. Nor is there agreement on the causes—Germany and Japan, some believe, were forced into their desperate moves by bumbling, uncomprehending statesmen of their enemies. However, if one single cause is required, none serves better than the German dictator, Adolf Hitler.

The Versailles Treaty, imposed on a vanquished Germany after World War I in 1919, is frequently cited as the underlying cause of the misery and discontent that produced a Hitler; that plus the vindictiveness of the French, the detachment of the British, and, eventually, the isolationism of the United States. The Great Depression, which devastated the American economy in 1929, had spread to Europe by the 1930s, compounding the postwar wretchedness and bitterness there.

In another part of the world, in a period when its home politics were rife with political assassinations, Japan began flexing its international muscles under a government dominated by the military. By 1931, implemented by a staged explosion in a railroad station at Mukden, China, the Japanese Army invaded the region of Manchuria; in February of the next year the Japanese established a puppet government there, renaming the province Manchukuo. Significantly, perhaps, this new Japanese "state" was recognized in the west by only two governments, Germany and Italy.

The term "fascism," popularly representing all that was evil in Hitler's Germany, was in fact coined in Italy. It was the political answer to Italy's economic woes of the early 1920s proffered by an ex-Socialist, writer, and teacher, Benito Mussolini, who dreamed of the rebirth of the Roman Empire.

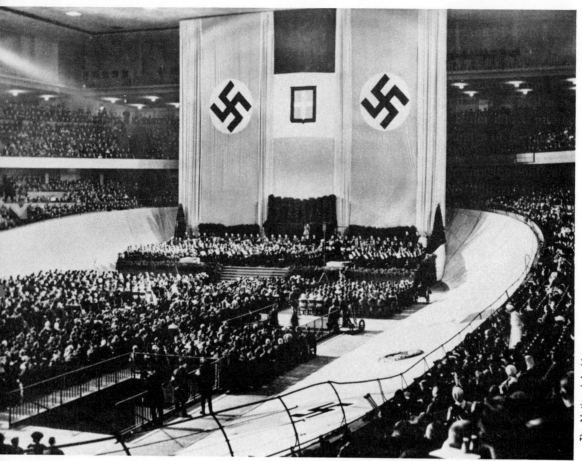

The National Archives

Cultural celebration of the Rome-Berlin Axis: a concert in Berlin honoring the Italian Army. Not long after, Germany and Japan formed the Anti-Comintern Pact; the contenders and issues of the next war were established.

By the crucial year 1929 a Fascist government was in control of Italy with Mussolini officially Il Duce (the leader). Mussolini, therefore, was the first European dictator upon the international scene; he would also make the first move toward war—the invasion of Ethiopia (Abyssinia) in October 1935.

Hitler, who in 1935 appeared to be a junior partner in what would be known as the "Rome-Berlin Axis," had begun his own moving and shaking. His once tiny and despised Nationalist Socialist German Workers' Party eventually emerged in the early 1930s as a major political force. By 1933 Hitler was reluctantly named Chancellor of Germany by senile and failing President Paul von Hindenburg.

Adolf Hitler and, momentarily, his senior partner-dictator, Benito Mussolini, shedding benevolence upon the populace.

Upon Hindenburg's death in 1934, Hitler merged the offices of Chancellor and President and pronounced himself the Fuehrer of the German Reich. The Nazis (from *Nationalsozialist*) united a majority of the German people in a denunciation of the Versailles Treaty, communism, and in a persecution of the Jews.

In March 1935, Hitler sent out his first signal when he publicly reviled the Versailles Treaty, particularly those clauses restricting German rearmament. The world was stunned, having assumed that since 1918 German military ambitions had been moribund. Actually, immediately following the Armistice a group of German military leaders, led by Hans von Seeckt, conspired to keep the infamous German General Staff alive and functioning secretly. With the aid of Soviet Russia, Seeckt and com-

15

Familiar newsreel shot of the Thirties: Hitler triumphantly entering an annexed addition to Germany's Lebensraum. *Local Nazis covered the streets with flowers.*

pany maintained a skeletal organization, began to build a new German air force and to develop a new concept in tank warfare.

Hitler, therefore, did not start from military scratch and, while his strength was never what the democracies imagined it to be, he soon revealed a gift for exaggeration that kept them off balance. Those leaders in France, Britain, and Russia who hoped to contain Hitler's military adventures were certain his army and air force could overwhelm them. So there was a tendency among the French and British leadership to bend to Hitler's will.

Hitler continued to chew up the Versailles Treaty. In March 1936 he made his first overt move: German troops marched into the Rhineland, a demilitarized buffer zone between Germany and France, Belgium and Luxembourg. Hitler gave as his reason a recently signed Franco-Russian pact; the French, overestimating Hitler's army and especially his air force, and getting no reassurances from their allies, did nothing.

16

Hapless symbol of appeasement, British Prime Minister Neville Chamberlain, invariably hoodwinked by Hitler, was fated to bring his nation into war with Germany.

Meanwhile, the war in Ethiopia had gone its predictable, uneven course. Mussolini's forces fought tribesmen armed with obsolete weapons, even spears, with the latest armaments: tanks and trucks, aircraft, and the leftover from World War I, poison gas. Mussolini's son Vittorio, a pilot, did not endear himself when he described the bombing of Ethiopian cavalry as "great sport."

The "sport" came to an end on May 5, 1936, when Italian troops occupied Addis Ababa, a victory for Mussolini and fascism.

That small conflagration had barely flickered out when another, a civil war, flared up in Spain. While it appeared to be a local dispute, the

Hitler's final touch: the 1939 Non-Aggression Pact with his archenemy, Communist Russia. With Hitler and an interpreter is Russian Foreign Minister Vyacheslav Molotov, who represented Stalin in an agreement that set the scene for World War II.

Spanish Civil War provided a testing ground for the latest battle techniques of the Luftwaffe (the German Air Force), for Hitler sent aid to Fascist leader General Francisco Franco; so did Mussolini. Russia sent aid, and weapons, to the Loyalists—and volunteers from other nations, including the United States, went off to Spain to fight, mostly on the Loyalist side. The new techniques of modern warfare were tried out on the Spanish earth and its people as the democracies watched Europe dividing into two main camps of future contenders—the Communists vs. the Fascist/Nazis.

Through 1937, Europe seethed but without any large-scale outbreak; international attention was drawn to the Far East. Using a minor clash between Chinese and Japanese troops at the Marco Polo Bridge near Peiping (now Peking) as an excuse, Japan initiated a full-scale invasion of Northern China in July. "We came to teach the Chinese a lesson," one Japanese commander was quoted as saying while Japanese troops swept through China, raping, killing, and looting. By autumn most of Northern China was held by the Japanese. In November, Italy joined

Germany and Japan in the Anti-Comintern Pact. On December 12, Americans received their first shock from the Far East, when Japanese aircraft attacked three American tankers, escorted by a Navy gunboat, *Panay,* on the Yangtze River below Nanking. Japan paid an indemnity of more than two million dollars for the *Panay* attack; it could not afford to break off relations with the United States, the source of all of Japan's scrap metal and steel, as well as two thirds of its oil.

In February 1938, Hitler added another title to the string he already had: Supreme Commander of the armed forces of Germany. He began to move again.

His first coup was primarily political, although military threats were implied: the *Anschluss* (union) with Austria. Nazi influence in Austria, after Hitler's coming to power, had made it a festering trouble spot of street brawls, killings, and bombings. Hitler, seeking to "preserve the racial community," began to inflame the infection by demanding that German-speaking Austrians be permitted to join the Fatherland. He also raised the question of *Lebensraum* (living space), which, he said, the Germans deserved more than any other people.

With German troops poised at the Austrian border, Hitler bulldozed Austrian Chancellor Kurt von Schuschnigg into a resignation, clearing the way for the Nazi Minister of Interior to replace him. Upon his appointment the new Chancellor, Arthur Seyss-Inquart, invited German troops to occupy Austria. Hitler was welcomed in Vienna with cries of *Ein Volk, ein Reich, ein Fuehrer!* (One people, one state, one leader!), cheers, and other words that must have been music to his ears: "Down with the Jews!" "Down with the Catholics!" and *"Heil Hitler!"* Could six million Austrians be wrong?

Hitler soon announced that no more territorial acquisitions concerned him, but—in truth—Czechoslovakia was next. He started with the Sudetenland, on Germany's eastern frontier, known for a vociferous German population clamoring to be reunited with Germany. The German Sudetens, a minority, accused the Czechs of persecution, giving Hitler his excuse to save the abused Germans, *his* Germans. The annexation did not come off as smoothly as the first *Anschluss;* the Czechs chose to resist, and Britain and France, although militarily not ready, raised objections.

Diplomacy was, of course, an alluring alternative to war, and a frenetic period ensued culminating at Munich. In their desperate and fruitless attempts to deal with Hitler, British Prime Minister Neville Chamberlain and French Premier Édouard Daladier went down in history as crass appeasers (at the same time they were undoubtedly cynically—or realistically—looking out for the collective necks of their respective nations).

Chamberlain and Daladier were bullied, lied to, and threatened with a European war ("a matter of complete indifference to me," Hitler said,

Tomorrow the world: Hitler and company at a state occasion. From right: Admiral Erich Raeder (in profile), commander of Germany's naval forces; Field Marshal Walther von Brauchitsch, planner of the invasion of Poland; Nazi Minister of Foreign Affairs (with back to camera) Joachim von Ribbentrop and Hitler.

"by next Monday we shall be at war."). When Chamberlain flew home from Munich (and he detested flying) on September 30, 1938, he carried a paper that he, Daladier, and Hitler had signed. Hitler had promised that he had made the "last territorial demand that I have to make in Europe," and so, despite Czech objections and the fact that no representative of their government participated in the talks, the Sudetenland was handed over to Germany. War had been averted and Chamberlain was greeted at the airport by a cheering crowd. "I believe," he told them as he displayed a copy of the agreement, "it is peace in our time."

One British voice had not joined in the cheering. Britain and France, Winston Churchill somberly informed the nation, "have sustained a total and unmitigated defeat . . . And I do not suppose this is the end. This is only the beginning of the reckoning . . ."

20

Within three weeks of the occupation of the Sudetenland, Hitler advised his military staff to draw up plans for "the liquidation of the remainder of Czechoslovakia." While this was going on the Nazis continued to incite Slovakia to break away as a German protectorate. Then Hitler summoned elderly President Emil Hácha to Berlin, where he was offered a choice between a German invasion or signing away his nation as a German protectorate. He was also treated to one of Hitler's classic temper tantrums and then literally chased around the conference table with the treaty and pen. Hácha fainted under the pressure, was revived by an injection, and finally signed the document. On March 16, 1939, Adolf Hitler, the conquerer, the self-proclaimed "Protector of Bohemia and Moravia," rode through the streets of Prague.

While the Hácha-signed paper lent a certain legality to this conquest, it caused reassessments within the international communities. The French Assembly granted Daladier the power to speed up rearmament. Neville Chamberlain went so far as to suggest that Hitler's word was not worth much. The American Ambassador was summoned home from Berlin.

Unimpressed, Hitler sent his troops marching into Memel, to bite off a little slice of Lithuania. He began making demands of Poland. The Versailles Treaty had taken a strip of land separating East Prussia from Germany proper and had given it to Poland. Known as the Polish Corridor, it provided landlocked Poland with access to the sea at Danzig. Hitler wanted Danzig.

On March 23, the day after the taking of Memel, Poland rejected Hitler's proposals on Danzig. On March 28, the day the Spanish Civil War ended with Fascist Dictator Franco the victor, Hitler denounced a German-Polish treaty dating from 1934.

Chamberlain then announced on March 31 that if Poland were attacked Britain and France would honor their agreements with that country (Chamberlain may have been counting on a second Munich at Danzig). Hitler reacted with screaming fury and ordered his generals to plan for the destruction of Poland.

In May, Germany and Italy signed their so-called "Pact of Steel," which united the two dictatorships militarily, at least on paper (Mussolini informed Hitler that, in fact, Italy was not yet prepared for a large-scale war). The pact removed Mussolini as a possible arbitrator between Britain and France and Germany.

August brought the diplomatic bombshell of the year: the German-Russian Non-Aggression Pact (which contained secret clauses pertaining to the partition of Poland between the signatories). This alliance between natural enemies was yet another staggering Hitlerian coup.

"Now," he exulted, "I have the world in my pocket!"

EUROPE
1939

NORWAY

SWEDEN

Helsinki

— SCAPA FLOW

Oslo

Stockholm

MANNERHEIM
LINE

KARELIAN
ISTHMUS
NOV. 30/39

GULF OF FINLAND

ESTONIA

BALTIC
SEA

LATVIA

Riga

NORTH SEA

LITHUANIA

Memel
MAR. 23/39

ENGLAND

London

NETHERLAND

Wilhelmshaven

Berlin

Danzig

EAST
PRUSSIA

POLISH CORRIDOR

OCT. 17/39

ENGLISH CHANNEL

BEF
SEPT. 10/39

BELGIUM

SIEGFRIED LINE

GERMANY

Posen

Warsaw

P O L A N D

ARDENNES

RHINE R.

Weimar

ELBE R.

SEPT. 1/39

VISTULA R.

LUXEMBOURG

RHINE-
LAND

MAGINOT
LINE

Paris

Prague

SUDETENLAND
MAR. 16/39

BOHEMIA & MORAVIA
MAR. 16/39

Lwow

CZECHOSLOVAKIA

SEINE R.

DANUBE R.

Munich

ANCHLUSS
1938

Vienna

LOIRE R.

F R A N C E

AUSTRIA

Budapest

SWITZERLAND

HUNGARY

ROMANIA

RHÔNE R.

PO R.

Belgrade

DANUBE R.

YUGOSLAVIA

BULG

I T A L Y

ADRIATIC
SEA

ALBANIA

N

SPAIN

Rome

CORSICA

GREECE

APR. 7/39

SARDINIA

MEDITERRANEAN SEA

SICILY

0	Miles	200
0	Km.	200

Pre-war Frontiers

palacios

1939
The Crime of War

IN THE early morning of September 1, 1939, German troops began moving swiftly across the Polish border. They had good reason; an "incident" staged for Hitler by German Intelligence: the attack by "Polish" troops on the German radio station at Gleiwitz. A Nazi SS (Schutzstaffel-secret police) leader broadcast a provoking speech in Polish and left dead soldiers (actually German prisoners) behind as he fled the scene.

What followed was the first full-scale demonstration of *blitzkrieg* (lightning war), in fact a British conception that had been ignored in Britain. Mechanized columns, spearheaded by *panzer* (tank) units smashed through the Polish frontiers in the north across the Polish Corridor, in the south from the newly acquired "protectorate," Czechoslovakia, and in the center from Germany itself—all columns snaking inexorably toward Warsaw. The panzers had been preceded by Luftwaffe bombers (Stuka dive bombers, in fact, had begun bombing important bridges five minutes ahead of Hitler's schedule). The bombers sweeping ahead of the ground troops struck at Polish airfields, railroads, bridges, and other lines of communication. The keynote was speed and, unencumbered by the marching infantry of the previous war, the blitzkrieg slashed into Poland along a wide front, from the Carpathian Mountains in the south to the Baltic Sea in the north.

While the attack was not unexpected, its impact was overwhelming as seemingly invincible and well-armed German troops poured through a dozen breaches in the Polish lines. The Poles chose to oppose with tried and true tactics and the weapons of another war. Horse cavalry was no match for columns of tanks, and yet reports came in of Polish attacks on panzers, on horseback and with drawn swords. Obsolete Polish aircraft were not a problem to the Luftwaffe. And the Polish High Command,

23

unprepared for a blitzkrieg, concentrated their main force in the wrong sector (near the Corridor; the rest of the forces were thinly spread southward where, in fact, lay the objective of the main German attack). There was also a misplaced dependence upon the help that might be forthcoming from their allies, Britain and France.

With German forces already established inside Poland, Chamberlain sent an ultimatum from London on September 2: get out of Poland or else.

Hitler ignored this unexpected strong language from the formerly complaisant Chamberlain.

Speaking from 10 Downing Street, Chamberlain, in a voice tinged with sadness and fatigue, said in a broadcast: "This morning the British Ambassador in Berlin handed the German Government a final note stating that, unless we heard from them by eleven o'clock that they were prepared to withdraw their troops from Poland, a state of war would exist between us. I have to tell you now that . . . consequently this country is at war with Germany."

Britain, joined by Australia, New Zealand, and France, declared war on Germany on September 3. On the same day Hitler invited Russia to begin earning its half of Poland, but Stalin demurred. The suddenness of the blitzkrieg had caught the Russians off balance also. Poland continued its losing battle alone. French General Maurice Gamelin intimated that his forces were engaging the Germans on land and in the air—but this was not true. Gamelin was hopefully awaiting the arrival of his British allies, who, in turn, were no more anxious than any of the other belligerents to expand the war.

Working in concert with the Stukas, German mobile units, using fast-moving tanks, moved quickly into Poland.

The National Archives

Harbingers of war: the Junkers Ju-87 Stuka dive bomber. Aircraft of this type struck the first military blow of World War II.

The British Royal Air Force struck its first blow of the war on September 4. Twenty-nine bombers were dispatched to attack German warships in the North Sea bases at Schillig Roads and Wilhelmshaven.

The mission was characteristically tentative, courageous, and ineffectual. The orders were explicit: the bombers were not to drop one bomb on land, only warships, in order to spare German civilians. They were further handicapped by miserable flying weather. And, they soon learned, such targets were ringed with murderous antiaircraft guns (flak). Consequently, seven British bombers never returned from that first raid and very little damage was done to the German warships.

After the fact: Hitler in the German Reichstag announcing the declaration of war on Poland. By this time German forces were already deep inside Poland's borders.

Bombs fall from an He-111 into Warsaw.

Such raids had no effect in Poland, where the *Wehrmacht* (the German Army) encircled and crushed the remnants of the Polish armies. Polish aerial activity had all but ceased. The infantry, without direction, fought in confusion and despair.

A disconcerted Stalin realized the time had come for him to move, for what appeared to be an unconquerable German army was headed his way. On September 17, Russian armies began crossing Poland's eastern border, encountering minimal resistance. The next day the Polish Commander in Chief, Marshal Edward Śmigly-Rydz, and Polish President Ignacy Mościcki and other government officials fled southward, between the German and Russian squeeze, to Rumania.

Within two days of the Soviet advance Polish resistance was sporadic, the little pockets quickly erased by Stukas or panzers. On September 25, Warsaw was heavily attacked in the first large-scale aerial bombardment of a major city in the twentieth century. Only 400 aircraft participated, but many flew several missions, raining down high explosives and incendiaries on the stubborn defenders of Warsaw. With meager Polish air opposition, the clumsy Stukas and even clumsier Junkers 52 transports flew over the city unchallenged, stoking the already burning rubble.

Warsaw surrendered on September 27; three days later a Polish Government in Exile was formed in Paris with General Wladyslaw Sikorski as Premier. The last of the Polish fighting flickered out by October 6.

The division of Poland was defined by a Russian-German "Treaty of Friendship." The boundary line ran roughly along the Curzon Line of 1920. In effect, in 1939, it placed the predominantly Polish-speaking

The results of German bombing of Warsaw; such bombing, and the invasion of Poland from the east by Russia, made further resistance impossible. Warsaw surrendered on September 27.

Embassy of the Polish People's Republic

population under German domination; the Russians took over the areas in which White Russians, Ukrainians, and Lithuanians predominated. The agreement also provided for an agreement as to Russia's "sphere of influence" in the Baltic countries on its western flank—Lithuania, Latvia, Estonia, and Finland.

Three of the pressured Baltic states readily complied; the single holdout was Finland. Soviet demands for a base on the Finnish mainland, islands in the Gulf of Finland, and a strip of land across the Karelian Isthmus, separating Finland and Russia, were discussed (these were not considered unreasonable demands, by the way). By late November, following fruitless talks, it was obvious that the Finns would not bend. Taking a leaf from Hitler's book, Stalin staged an "incident" on the Karelian Isthmus: an artillery attack on Russian positions by the Finns. This provided the justification for canceling the Finnish-Russian Pact that had been signed only on the previous September 29. On November 30 heavy Russian ground fire along the Russo-Finnish border and a heavy aerial attack on Helsinki raised the curtain on the "Winter War."

Meanwhile, on the Western Front the section of the French border that touched Germany was fortified by the legendary Maginot Line ("impenetrable" was a favorite adjective of the time; "immobile" was a more appropriate one with the advent of blitzkrieg). The line had not

Imperial War Museum, London

The Stuka was capable of quite accurate bombing because it could dive at the target and release its bombs and make a quick pullout. Its shrieking noise was nearly as frightening as its bombload.

The German "pocket battleship" Graf Spee, *built in accordance with the restrictions of the Versailles Treaty (which forbade German battleships). The* Graf Spee *was fast, well gunned, and sank eight ships in the South Atlantic (and one in the Indian Ocean) in the early months of the war.*

been extended northward along the Belgian border because of Belgian objections (they were not the natural enemies of the French) and because the French High Command did not believe that the Germans were capable of pushing an attack through Belgium because of the equally impenetrable Ardennes Forest.

Britain and France needed time to mobilize their conscript armies while the German armies moved into Poland. On September 10 a British Expeditionary Force, under Lord John Standish Gort, began moving across the English Channel into France. The French, mobilizing, were not capable of military movement until September 17. The French commanders, their thinking circumscribed by the classic set pieces of the Great War, hoped to begin their attack with a massive artillery barrage —but it took time to get the guns out of storage and made ready for firing. The French by this time had made a gentle, five-mile, penetration into Germany. By September 27 the movement of the BEF from England had been completed: two divisions, some 250,000 men. Gamelin, as Commander in Chief of the Allied Forces, ordered them to take positions along the Belgian frontier.

But by this time it was apparent that Poland was a lost cause. On October 24, Gamelin ordered those French troops that had invaded Germany back to France. Many of the reserves that had by this time been called to arms were placed in the Maginot Line and waited for something to happen. What followed was a period of deceptive calm which

Finnish ski troops move through an evergreen forest to harass the Russian Army.

would be called with cynical disdain by American politicians and newspapermen the "Phony War."

While this *Sitzkrieg,* which apparently disappointed the bloodthirsty, ensued, the war at sea began with German submarines drawing first blood. These revived echoes of World War I: the brutal Hun and his hated *Unterseeboot.* On September 4, the day after Britain declared war on Germany, the liner *Athenia,* bound from Liverpool to Montreal and carrying 1,400 passengers, was attacked without warning and sunk by U-30. Among the 112 *Athenia* dead were 28 Americans.

The first military loss was the British aircraft carrier *Courageous,* sent to the bottom by another German U-boat two weeks later. On October 14, under the command of *Leutnant* Guenther Prien, U-47 slipped into the great British naval base at Scapa Flow and torpedoed the battleship *Royal Oak,* with heavy loss of life, and slipped out again undetected. This was a powerful psychological setback, a British naval defeat in home waters.

German U-boats and aircraft also mined various sea approaches to Britain, greatly complicating the problem of imports on which the British depended so heavily.

The war on British shipping was not confined to home waters. By the end of September it was known that the German "pocket battleship" *Admiral Graf Spee* had begun a most successful hunting career in the South Atlantic by sinking the merchant ship *Clement* off the coast of Brazil. Early in the morning of December 13, the *Graf Spee* encountered a weak force of three British cruisers, no match for the heavily gunned and fast pocket battleship, off the coast of Uruguay. Despite his orders not to engage with the British unless necessary, Captain Hans Langsdorff opened fire. The heavy guns of the *Graf Spee* forced the *Exeter,* with heavy casualties and severe damage, out of the battle.

The two smaller cruisers, *Achilles* and *Ajax,* continued the duel—fire from their 6-inch guns against the *Graf Spee*'s 11-inch missiles. The battle lasted a hundred minutes and both British ships, badly damaged, broke off the battle. But the *Graf Spee* had also suffered, and Langsdorff turned the ship away from the cripples and fled up the River Plate to the neutral port of Montevideo, where he hoped to repair the damage and arrange for the burial of his 36 dead.

While the British ships waited off the estuary of the Plate (to be joined subsequently by a heavy cruiser), Langsdorff was caught between two jaws of a diplomatic/military vise: the Uruguayan authorities (who were anti-Nazi) would not grant him enough time to repair the *Graf Spee,* and his orders from Berlin were that he was not to suffer internment in Uruguay. A third pressure was applied by British propaganda, which led Langsdorff to believe that the ships awaiting his departure from Montevideo included an aircraft carrier.

The Graf Spee *burns in the River Plate after being scuttled by its crew; the captain, Hans Langsdorff, later committed suicide.*

The National Archives

By December 17, Langsdorff had made his decision. His time had run out and, with a minimal crew (he had left most of the crew behind with some 300 prisoners taken from the ships he had sunk), he guided the *Graf Spee* out of port, and, once out of the main channel, ran it aground. Langsdorff then scuttled the ship with a spectacular explosion. Three days later he concluded the drama, which was avidly reported in the newspapers of the time, by shooting himself.

There was little for newspapers to report from the Western Front as 1939 came to a close, however. Hitler's perfunctory peace offer made to the Allies had been rejected in October, and shortly after he revealed his future military plans to his General Staff. They were appalled. Hitler planned an autumn attack upon the Anglo-French forces, including a movement through neutral Belgium to skirt the Maginot Line.

Hitler's military advisers, in turn, tried to impress him with the fact that, despite the surprising victory over Poland, their armies were smaller than those of the Allies, and that some German units were poorly armed. They feared also that enlarging the war could lead to a world war. Secretly some members of the High Command had begun thinking about overthrowing Hitler. But neither the attack nor the deposition of Hitler occurred. The proposed invasion of France and Belgium was postponed several times by bad weather and eventually cancelled. This, in turn, rendered the overthrow unnecessary.

It was the war in Finland that captured the attention of the world. The Russians had seriously misjudged the Finns, the terrain of Finland, and the near-arctic weather. Certain of victory, the massed Russian armies attacked across the Karelian Isthmus only to be mowed down at the Mannerheim Line (named for Baron Carl Gustaf von Mannerheim).

All along the Finnish border Russian armies moved into thick forests covered with snow and concealing the *Bielaja Smert* ("White Death," Finnish commandos, on skis and dressed in white, who seemed to appear out of nowhere to harass the Russians, cut their supply lines, and disappear into the whiteness). Snipers made the lighting of campfires in the subzero weather suicidal, and Russian soldiers froze to death in countless numbers.

The struggle of brave "little Finland" standing up to the Soviet giant captured the imagination and sympathy of the world that winter of 1939. A heroic people, a nation of four million, was winning over an aggressor that had a population of two hundred million to draw upon. Obviously the Soviet military machine was not what it was cracked up to be. This was a miscalculation shared by the Allies and Hitler.

Remnants of a Polish horse-drawn unit following a Stuka attack.

The Luftwaffe approaches beleaguered Warsaw; a gunner's view from the nose of a Heinkel He-111.

*Poland, September 1, 1939—German troops inside a Polish village,
clearing the houses of snipers.*

The victors: Commander in Chief of the German Army High Command, Field Marshal Walther von Brauchitsch and his Supreme Commander, Hitler.

Commander of Army Group South in its plunge into Poland, General Gerd von Rundstedt, one of the last representatives of the old German General Staff that survived World War I.

A Polish girl mourns her sister after German aircraft had strafed a refugee-crowded road.

Warsaw was reduced to rubble in history's first large-scale bombing of a major city.

Inception of Hitler's "Final Solution": Polish-Jewish slave laborers working under the direction of the Schutzstaffel, the infamous "SS." Originally formed as a private guard for Hitler, the SS became the major dispenser of Nazi frightfulness in occupied countries and German concentration camps.

Hitler's unexpectedly quick conquest of Poland unnerved Stalin, who moved into Russia's "sphere of influence" to protect the Russian northern flank. He was successful in the Baltic states but ran into serious resistance from tiny Finland. Trained Finnish troops, as seen here, proved more than a match for the then poorly led and equipped great Russian Army.

Inevitably, the Russians were victors in the Russo-Finnish war—but not until the Red Army paid heavily. Finnish troops have come upon a frozen Russian soldier.

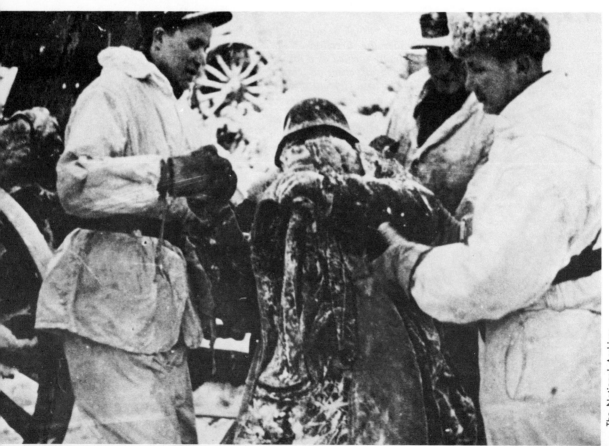

Despite the heroic effort by the Finns, the Red Army by sheer numbers overwhelmed the tiny Finnish defense and burst into Finland. In the path of the invader, this Finnish home burns to the ground.

Baron Carl Gustaf Mannerheim, soldier-statesman who organized Finnish defenses against the Russian invasion. The famed "Mannerheim Line" across the Karelian Isthmus held off two large Russian armies for several weeks.

1940

Lone Britannia

THE YEAR BEGAN with heavy Russian attacks on the Karelian Isthmus, resulting in the destruction of the Russian 44th Division. At the same time, although the Allies seemed none too concerned with the probability, Hitler continued to press his generals for an attack in the West.

Then on January 10 a small plane flying a liaison officer, Major Helmut Reinberger, from Münster to Bonn ran into bad weather and was blown off course and forced to land. In his briefcase he carried the complete operational plans for Hitler's proposed attack in the West.

As fate would have it, the major's little plane had been blown into Belgium. Reinberger's attempts to burn the highly secret papers were unsuccessful and, though charred, they fell into Belgian hands. That evening King Leopold III had a long telephone conversation with Wilhelmina, Queen of the Netherlands. Obviously their tiny nations figured in the German plans for the Western offensive. Soon word was leaked to the Allies, although the Allies were still denied permission to move through Belgian territory.

There were howls in the German camp, although no one had any idea of just how much had been revealed by the unburned portion of the papers. Hitler was calm, however. He again canceled the order for the attack in the West—the set date had been January 17—for a new plan had already been suggested. The brainchild of General Erich von Manstein, the plan was more daring than the original one prepared by Hitler's General Staff, which shifted the main thrust of the offensive from central Belgium to the "impenetrable" Ardennes Forest in the south (which required an invasion of neutral Luxembourg and Belgium). Although opposed by German military traditionalists, the Manstein Plan was embraced by Hitler—but not until after Reinberger's mis-

41

Norway's rugged terrain did not lend itself to the modern blitzkrieg. A German supply column moves up using an ancient means of transportation.

fortune. (Later, when the plan succeeded even beyond Manstein's expectations, Hitler took credit for its conception. He threw Manstein a crumb. "Among all the generals I talked to about the new plan in the West," he recalled, "Manstein was the only one who understood me.")

At the same time Hitler kept a wary eye on the northern battleground and another on Britain's First Lord of the Admiralty, Winston Churchill. The pugnacious old sea dog had begun to urge the British Cabinet to authorize the mining of Norwegian territorial waters in hopes of "stopping the Norwegian transportation of Swedish iron-ore from Narvik" to the German war industries. Hitler's wary eye also took in the antics of his ally-for-the-moment, Stalin. Although Russian chances there seemed poor, it would be only a matter of time before its seemingly unlimited mass of arms and men would crush the tiny Finnish Army. That would place the Soviets within reach of the Gällivare iron-ore deposits in Sweden.

Hitler hoped for Scandinavian neutrality, but the stirrings in the north disconcerted him. He was aware of the importance of keeping the supply line from Narvik open, especially in the winter, when the southern Swedish ports were closed in and the Gulf of Bothnia was frozen. He gave only the slightest consideration to Grand Admiral Erich Raeder, Commander in Chief of the German Navy, who instructed Hitler in the importance of establishing naval bases, especially for submarines, along the Norwegian coast.

Early in February the Allied Supreme Council met in Paris to discuss military aid to Finland (Chamberlain was accompanied by Churchill). Britain was to provide two divisions and the French a somewhat lesser force in a purportedly volunteer "Aid to Finland" mission, only a fraction of which was to proceed to Finland beyond Gällivare. A date was set for early March.

Then an unexpected incident occurred to galvanize Hitler into a Scandinavian reaction. In February 16, British destroyers had pursued the German supply ship *Altmark* (certain that it was carrying British prisoners who had survived the sinkings by the *Graf Spee*), which fled into Norwegian waters to take refuge in Jøsenfjord. The Norwegians, eager to maintain neutrality, assured the British that, upon inspection, no British prisoners had been found. Under Churchill's orders, Captain Philip Vian, aboard the destroyer *Cossack,* was instructed to enter Norwegian waters and to board the *Altmark*. Despite protests from the Norwegian Government and the presence of two gunboats, Vian pushed into Jøsenfjord, ordered his men to search the *Altmark,* and found 299 captured British merchant seamen hidden in locked storerooms and empty oil drums.

The German propaganda press condemned this British "crime," which was, indeed, a violation of Norwegian neutrality. At the same time, the Germans had hoodwinked the Norwegian inspectors by claiming that there were no British prisoners aboard and that the *Altmark* was unarmed (Vian's men found several guns in addition to the cramped prisoners). Of even greater importance: such a British interest in Scandinavia disturbed Hitler. On February 20 he summoned General Nikolaus von Falkenhorst and appointed him commander for an invasion of Norway; by the end of the month yet another country was added to the plan for conquest: Denmark.

By early March, Hitler had confirmed the invasion of Denmark and Norway (Operation Weserubung). The war in Finland was drawing to

Elverum, Norway, in the path of German forces that moved northward from Oslo, driving out the Anglo-French relief forces sent to aid Norway.

the predictable close: the Russian juggernaut had broken through the Mannerheim Line and on March 12 the Winter War ended with the signing of a Russo-Finnish pact in Moscow. The following day brought the signing of the Treaty of Moscow, granting Russia all it had demanded originally plus a little more. The Russian armies had won a small victory and lost a great deal of prestige. But, as one Soviet general commented, "We have won enough ground to bury our dead."

Next, as if of one mind, the Allies and Germany began maneuvering for favorable positions; each prepared to "save" Norway from the other. The Allies began first, with plans for landing troops in Norway as well as mining Norwegian waters (this last was accomplished on April 5). Two days later an Allied force sailed for Norway.

On April 9, Hitler pounced. Denmark capitulated, and was occupied, within hours of the launching of the attack. The Norwegians chose to resist.

Although no blitzkrieg, the Norwegian campaign was distinctive for a number of reasons. For the first time in modern warfare airborne troops were employed (German paratroopers were responsible for securing several strategically placed airfields); the German Navy made its one major contribution to Hitler's war-making (its losses to the Royal Navy during the fighting around Norway seriously crippled the German Fleet, curtailing any important action on its part in any invasion attempt on Britain); the Luftwaffe again played an important role in taking Norway and, once established in the Norwegian bases, was a threat to Britain from the northeast; it also flew over northern shipping lanes.

Like the Finns, the Norwegians fought bravely against a better-armed and numerous enemy. The Allies attempted to aid the Norwegians, but to no ultimate effect. French troops joined the Norwegians in the fighting of what now appears to have been a poorly planned campaign (Prime Minister Chamberlain, who endorsed the Norwegian adventure, actually Churchill's pet idea, would be blamed for the failure. This would lead to his resignation on a fatal day: May 10).

By June 8 all Allied troops that could be were withdrawn from Norway. The Germans had won the war there. By June 10, with the Norwegian Government and King Haakon VII transported to Britain, the capitulation of Norway was complete. The Luftwaffe had gained important bases in the north and the supply of Swedish iron ore was assured to Germany.

But even as the fighting raged in Norway, Hitler stunned the Allies with another blow: he ended the Phony War. Despite the doubts of his military advisers, Hitler ordered the offensive in the West to begin at dawn, Friday, May 10, 1940.

From the Netherlands in the north to tiny Luxembourg in the south, two German Army groups moved into Holland, Belgium, and France. A

The swastika in Oslo. The Norwegians fought a losing war from April until June, after which the country was occupied by Nazi forces.

third group, opposite the Maginot Line, would keep the French preoccupied there. Army Group B, under the command of General Fedor von Bock in the north, would appear to be making the main thrust through Holland. In the center General Gerd von Rundstedt's Army Group A would deliver the main blow through Belgium and Luxembourg—through the Ardennes, to the north of the Maginot Line. In addition to his regular infantry, Rundstedt also commanded three panzer corps. The plan, initiated by Manstein, was to throw off the defenses by appearing to make the traditional assault on France through Holland and northern Belgium, which would tie up the British Expeditionary Force and distract the French away from the Ardennes. At the same time the immobile Maginot Line would be given its due, engaged by the token Army Group C.

The attack opened on the right flank with terror and confusion for the defenders, as airborne troops began dropping out of the still-dark sky. Dummy paratroopers were planted throughout the area, making it impossible to predict where the main blow would fall. The Luftwaffe bombed and strafed, and delivered the airborne troops, who secured airfields and bridges across the Maas River into southern Holland. The same tactics were used in Belgium, with one dramatic innovation: the taking of the formidable Fort Eben Emael with a handful of men who landed atop the fort in gliders towed to the scene by the Luftwaffe.

45

Such spectacular feats drew the attention of the Allies to the right flank, while the German forces, spearheaded by the aggressive leadership of General Heinz Guderian and his XIX Panzer Corps, began rushing through Luxembourg and the Ardennes toward Sedan in France. It would take just long enough for the Allies' distraction to the north to make this main armored thrust all but invincible.

Within five days Holland was forced to capitulate and surrendered on May 15—the day following a notorious bombing attack on Rotterdam. This aerial assault would serve in the cause of anti-German propaganda for years to come. Even as the surrender of Rotterdam was being negotiated, on the fourteenth, a large formation of Heinkel (He-111) bombers appeared over the city. Of the hundred that had been dispatched, about half did not receive the recall order that canceled the mission. Nearly a hundred tons of bombs fell into the already stricken city as result of this error, reducing its rubble to pebbles. Great fires destroyed some 20,000 dwellings and, of course, lives.

The figure released at the time to a horrified world was 30,000 dead —men, women, and children. Rotterdam joined Guernica, Spain, and Warsaw, Poland, as a symbol of German military brutality.

Fort Eben Emael, Belgium, was like the Maginot Line, considered a formidable obstacle to the Wehrmacht. Instead of butting it head-on, the Germans took it from the air: airborne troops landed on the fort's plateau ignoring a 120-foot wall rising up from the Albert Canal. Engineer paratroopers, who have dealt with Eben Emael's defenses, celebrate with a break for a smoke.

Belgium continued fighting, but the outcome was obvious, and the Allies began seeking means of extricating themselves. On the day that Holland surrendered, German panzers to the south had already crossed the Meuse (Maas) River and were inside France. Guderian's armored forces had negotiated the seventy miles of the "impassable" Ardennes, pushed aside French resistance, and arrived at the river within four days. With the line broken, Guderian was followed by fifty divisions. And once the Meuse was crossed near Sedan, Guderian could deploy his forces across the French countryside, unconstricted by the Ardennes.

Counterattacks from the air proved fruitless, for the Luftwaffe controlled the air over the battlefronts. A French armored attack against Guderian's left flank was brushed aside readily with Luftwaffe assistance. This rare counterattack was led by a little-known general, Charles de Gaulle.

Guderian moved too fast even for the Germans. The High Command was concerned with his pushing too deeply into France, leaving his columns open to flanking attacks. How could the French permit such a thing without attempting a heavy counterstroke? What Guderian's superiors (and Guderian, too) did not know was that Premier Paul Reynaud had already called Winston Churchill (British Prime Minister since May 10, when Chamberlain had resigned) to inform him, "We are beaten; we have lost the battle!"

Disregarding the orders of his superiors, Guderian surged deeper into France and by May 20 had reached the Channel coast. Upon reaching the English Channel, Guderian had succeeded in cutting France in half and had begun to move behind the Allied armies facing the German forces to the north.

Churchill, hoping to bolster French morale, flew to Paris during the period, only to encounter despair. There was a shakeup in the French High Command, Gamelin was replaced by seventy-three-year-old General Maxime Weygand, a hero of World War I. Weygand, assuming a hopeless and confused undertaking, took on the new job with a cryptic but rallying statement. Tapping his briefcase, he sagely said, "I have the secrets of Marshal Foch." The briefcase, like the situation, was empty.

Churchill, persuasive as he was, could not salvage the Battle of France. He promised more fighter squadrons, but—happily for Britain later—was stubbornly resisted by the Royal Air Force head of Fighter Command, Air Chief Marshal Sir Hugh Dowding.

With Guderian moving around his back from the south and with Army Group B and its panzers pushing against him from the north, the commander of the BEF, Gort, cast anxious eyes on the treacherous but inviting English Channel. By May 25, when it seemed that all of Northern France was infested with German tanks or armored vehicles, Gort was certain that an evacuation of the British Expeditionary Force was inevitable. (Admiral Bertram Ramsay of the Royal Navy had begun formulating plans for just such an eventuality; with the Germans apparently invincible, no great hopes were held for the escape of great numbers.)

The final resistance of the Belgian Army enabled Gort to form a defensive line around the French coastal city of Dunkirk. The situation seemed hopeless. In order to carry off what would come to be called the "Miracle of Dunkirk," the British would require some higher help—and they got it from Hitler.

On May 24, the day before Gort had finally decided to evacuate his troops, Guderian had swung along the Channel coast cutting off escape ports and was closer to Dunkirk than the British. On this day Hitler himself ordered Guderian to stop, undoubtedly influenced by his own high command and recollections of the plains of Flanders of World War I.

Was Hitler's decision guided by cold feet or a warm heart? Since these traits had not characterized his character before, it seems unlikely that the well-being of the British Empire much concerned him. He may well have decided that he was pressing his luck a bit to permit the panzers to stretch their supply lines and to become more vulnerable to flanking counterattacks—and why not let the Luftwaffe add to its glory?

Whatever Hitler's true reason, he did call a halt to the panzer thrust toward Dunkirk for three days; in that period and until June 2 the British carried out their miracle.

During the night of May 26, Admiral Ramsay, commanding from Dover, set "Operation Dynamo" in motion. Beginning on May 27, while Allied troops held a perimeter around Dunkirk (two other ports, Boulogne and Calais, were in German hands), the little ships plied the dangerous and treacherous waters of the English Channel. Poor weather hampered rescue operations as well as the Luftwaffe and the RAF. For nine days Dynamo continued. The Luftwaffe proved to be less formidable than its leader Reich Marshal Hermann Goering had promised, and weather permitted full-scale operation only on three days. The German planes bombing and strafing the beaches, as well as the ships racing for Britain, were mauled by the RAF's Hurricanes and Spitfires.

The initial evacuations were disappointing, but by the third day, what with smoke covering the pickup areas, with clouds and reasonably smooth waters, the miracle blossomed. A great volunteer force united with Ramsay's armada—as pleasure yachts, Thames barges, French and Belgian fishing boats, tugs joined in the operation (of the 860 ships and boats that participated 243 were sunk with a loss of about 2,000 lives).

Ramsay's armada shipped only men; all equipment had to be abandoned—guns, vehicles, ammunition, supplies, most of it left burning on the beach by German air attacks.

But by June 2 the Germans had begun squeezing the perimeter with the release of the panzers. In the evening of June 3 the final attempt was made, resulting in the rescue of some 26,000 French troops, with 40,000 remaining behind to fight a rearguard action—and the survivors taken prisoner (a factor in the later Franco-British estrangement).

What was the Miracle of Dunkirk? There was heavy loss of life and prisoners taken, ships and aircraft were lost, and equipment and stores abandoned. When Operation Dynamo began, it was expected that perhaps, with luck, 45,000 troops might be evacuated. By the morning of June 4, when it was necessary to break off the operation, no less than 338,000 Allied troops had been taken from the smoking beaches.

Nor was Dunkirk a German victory for this very reason; true the British had been driven out of France, but their army and their will to fight had not been annihilated. But, that done, the Germans could turn to the French and the remaining British to the south. The forces moved southward and moved on the "Weygand Line," along the Somme and Aisne Rivers, where the French fought tenaciously against overwhelming odds. By June 7 panzers smashed through and began moving toward Rouen— by which time Weygand advised the government to ask for an armistice.

On June 10, Mussolini finally made his entry: he declared war on France and Britain, lest he miss out on the division of spoils. He would prove to be a thorn in Hitler's side.

On June 14, German troops entered Paris, declared an open city, and German armored units continued to race southward over a broad front. Two days later Reynaud resigned as Premier and a new government was formed under a veteran, hero of Verdun, Henri Philippe Pétain. The next day Pétain asked for armistice terms. On June 22, the armistice was signed at Compiègne in the same railway car in which the Germans had signed their armistice in 1918, which led to the Treaty of Versailles. It was a touch of Hitlerian irony.

Under the terms of the armistice, German troops would occupy all of Northern France, including Paris, and the Atlantic coast down to Spain. The government of France was moved south, into unoccupied France, and re-established at Vichy.

Rebel General de Gaulle chose to flee to Britain, where, with few followers and a gift for antagonizing his allies, he soon became the leader of the Free French. Shortly after, on July 3, the French-British estrangement was further aggravated when the Royal Navy, concerned over the probability of the French Fleet falling into Nazi hands, seized French warships in British ports and attacked a squadron of the French fleet at Oran, Algeria, resulting in crippling damages and a heavy loss of French lives. The next day Vichy France broke off diplomatic relations with Britain.

"What General Weygand called the Battle of France is over," Win-

Marshal Henri Philippe Pétain, hero of Verdun, greets the new conqueror of France. Pétain would head the government at Vichy, in southern unoccupied France.

All possible means of water transportation were drafted into use for Operation Dynamo, from ships of the Royal Navy to civilian pleasure boats and tugs. Not all reached Britain because of attacks by the Luftwaffe; smaller vessels were swamped by overcrowding. Despite this more than 300,000 British and French troops were rescued from Dunkirk.

"Operation Dynamo," the evacuation of Allied troops from France, under way. Allied troops awaiting shipping to take them off the Dunkirk beach.

ston Churchill informed his countrymen on June 18. "I expect that the Battle of Britain is about to begin." These were but two sentences in his celebrated "This was their finest hour" speech, in which he solemnly prepared the nation for the expected coming fury: the German invasion of Britain. The Battle of Britain did follow, but in an unexpected form —the first great, decisive air battle in history.

Although German air assaults had been expected from the very beginning of the war, as blackout restrictions were duly enforced, gas masks issued, mothers, children, and the infirm evacuated from the larger cities, the German bombers had not come during 1939, or the Phony War; nor was there any serious activity during the hectic Battle of France.

Hitler clung to the belief that the British, despite Churchill, would realize that they were in a "militarily hopeless position," and would make an honorable peace. At the same time he may have longed for an alliance with Britain for a holy war on Communist Russia. In July, in fact, Guderian's operational staff left France for Berlin to prepare for an assault on Russia.

There being no response to his "peace offerings" from Britain, Hitler ordered, on July 16, that preparations for a full-scale invasion be made

Hitler and entourage arrive at Compiègne, France, for the signing of the armistice and revenge for the Versailles Treaty. In the background, the railway car where the treaty would be signed—the same car in which Germany surrendered after World War I.

A later response to the German occupation, Free French English-trained commandos making a hit-and-run raid on the coast of Nazi-held France.

and ready for execution by mid-August. This operation was to be called "Sealion."

This new turn threw the German High Command into consternation. Admiral Raeder, whose war fleet had been badly mauled by the Royal Navy during the Scandinavian campaign, realized that he would have to arrange for the transportation of the invasion forces across the hated Channel. He had no fleet of landing craft at his disposal. The victorious ground forces only had to wait until Raeder could ferry them. The English Channel would have to be made safe for that passage—a job for Goering's Luftwaffe.

The Luftwaffe had been making incursions over Britain all through July, without much effect but with losses on both sides. It was, however, on August 1, 1940, that Hitler ordered the battle to begin with his secret Directive No. 17, which opened with the words: "The German Air Force is to overcome the English air forces with all means at its disposal and as soon as possible." He closed with the more specific "The air war may begin on August 5," adding that the "Navy is authorized to begin intensified operations on the same date."

If Raeder was perplexed and unprepared, and if the Army planners were willing to wait for transportation across the great antitank ditch, Goering was delighted: he was ready, willing, and unable. The

Luftwaffe would wipe out the Royal Air Force fighters in four days—in two weeks the air over the Channel would belong to Germany and Sealion could begin.

In Britain, preparations were under way for the expected invasion. Unarmed or ill-equipped members of the Home Guard were ready to fight to the last ditch in keeping with Churchill's motto, should invasion come: "You can always take one with you." The mood was grim but one of elation.

Although the Luftwaffe did not have the great air forces at its disposal that legend contends, it was an epic of heroism (on both sides) which in fact was decided by "the few" that Churchill would later memorialize. Each side had its advantages and handicaps, the worst of the Luftwaffe's being its top leadership, especially Goering, whose thinking was colored by the romanticism of the World War I dogfight. He had the scantiest understanding of the employment of air power.

Britain's leader of Fighter Command, on which the bulk of the battle would fall, was Goering's opposite. Stubborn, taciturn, undemonstrative, Sir Hugh Dowding understood the problems of men and machines in aerial combat; he was a brilliant strategist and administrator. Dowding —if one could assign so complex a thing to an individual—won the Battle of Britain.

There were many other factors: the British were operating over their home grounds—the Germans were flying from bases in the Low Countries and France, often to the limit of their fuel supplies. A British pilot could bail out of a plane and, if uninjured, be back in the battle the fol-

Pilots scramble to their Hurricanes to intercept Luftwaffe bombers.

lowing day (this was no rarity)—a German pilot would be taken prisoner. And Luftwaffe pilots, injured or in severely damaged aircraft, attempting to get back to home bases, often ended up in the English Channel with the chances of being captured, or rescued by German craft, less than equal.

Probably, aside from sheer human determination and courage, the greatest advantage the British had over the Germans was in the field of electronics—in the use of radar (a device that detected the approach of enemy aircraft even as they were forming up over France) and in intercommunications between the ground radar stations and pilots as well as pilot to pilot. It was possible to shift forces from enemy formation to enemy formation, thus conserving fighter strength for important incursions. While this did not always work to perfection, the use of radar in the battle was a decisive asset. It might be noted for the benefit of those who maintain that war is "man's work" that the hands, eyes, and minds of the personnel "manning" the important radar stations and working in RAF operations rooms belonged to the voluntary members of Britain's Women's Auxiliary Air Force—a number of whom would die at their posts during the battle.

Ringing Britain from Norway and Denmark in the north to, roughly, Normandy in the south were three great German air fleets (*Luftflotten*) with strength of about 3,000 aircraft, about a third of which were fighters. The impressive number does not tell the true tale, for only about two thirds of these aircraft were operational and available for the

Overture to the Blitz: an He-111 passes over London and the bend in the Thames on September 7, 1940. The war enters a new phase: the Germans had lost the Battle of Britain.

Imperial War Museum, London

assault. Fighter Command could muster about 700 fighters, Hurricanes and Spitfires.

The greater concentration of German aircraft was based opposite Southern England (which was the projected landing area for the invasion). The brunt of the Battle of Britain was taken by No. 11 Group, based in this area, just south and west of London. The group was commanded by a most capable New Zealander, Air Vice Marshal Sir Keith Park.

After a number of delays, Goering initiated his offensive. "Eagle Day," switched from August 10, 1940, was to take place on August 13. Poor weather got the operation off to a confused beginning, although the Luftwaffe struck at airfields and radar stations in southeast England.

Eagle Day seemed to indicate that the German objective was to clear a path to London by knocking out the RAF fighter fields in between.

This was confirmed on August 15. All three Luftflotten participated, including the more distant Luftflotte 5, stationed in Norway and Denmark. Poorly escorted by a few twin-engine Messerschmitt Me-110s, the bomber formations were badly mauled by British fighters of No. 13 Group, based in Northern England. One German formation lost 15 planes at no cost to the RAF; a second formation, although successful in striking a bomber base, lost 10 planes. This proved to be the sole daytime contribution of Luftflotte 5 to the Battle of Britain, at a great cost to the Germans.

More heavily protected bombers to the south concentrated on air bases and with much success. But British radar, when not confused by great numbers of aircraft, did send Hurricanes and Spitfires to meet the formations (one containing as many as 200 German planes).

The German bombers inflicted severe damage on several airfields, but at a great cost. The RAF claimed no less than 182 German aircraft, more an indication of the intensity of that day's fighting rather than to a lack of candor. The actual German loss for the day numbered 75—no small number. The RAF lost 34 aircraft.

By August 17, Goering's four days were up; the skies over England, and more importantly over the Channel, were not cleared of the RAF. There was an uneasiness in the German camp; more fighter protection would be assigned to the bombers, and no Stuka could venture out without heavy escort. The Me-110 had not proved to be the superfighter that Goering had hoped for; he also made a fateful decision. He ordered the Luftwaffe to stop attacking radar sites "in view of the fact that not one of those attacked so far has been put out of action." This was not true, but Goering was not aware of it.

Nor was he aware of the effects of the several days of fighting on hard-pressed Fighter Command. Replacement pilots were not always available to fill in for those killed or injured (it was easier to replace the aircraft). Fatigue from the strain of day-after-day fighting took its toll.

Goering's war on the RAF was more potent than he knew. Luftwaffe crews, however, were tired also—and discouraged. Because of a prewar error in Intelligence, plus the great number of British aircraft claimed as destroyed, aircrews were astonished to see more British fighters to challenge them when there should have been less. German Intelligence, at least the Luftwaffe's, was not characterized by Teutonic efficiency. For example, after the great battle of August 15, Intelligence calculated that only 300 operational British aircraft remained; in fact, there were more than twice that number.

RAF pilot attrition was becoming a serious problem, when an accident changed the course of the Battle. During a night raid a formation of about ten German bombers, off course, dropped their bombs by mistake on London.

An aroused Churchill ordered a reprisal raid the following night on Berlin. A formation of 80 British bombers complied, but with no great effect militarily. Goering, however, was affronted, for he had promised that no enemy aircraft would be permitted to fly over the Third Reich. Hitler, enraged, promised to erase British cities off the map.

So it was at the point at which the Luftwaffe had all but worn down Fighter Command by the series of attacks on their bases and other installations that the concentration was shifted from the airfields in Southern England to London.

The airfield assaults continued for a few more days, and then on Saturday, September 7, the period that would come to be called the "Blitz" began with a massive daylight attack on London. This unexpected turn was initially misread as the beginning of the invasion (barges and other landing craft had been spotted accumulating in German-held Channel ports). But the invasion did not come.

The morning after: No. 23 Victoria Street, London, falls burning after a German night raid on the city.

Winston Churchill, British Prime Minister following the resignation of Chamberlain, doughty symbol of the British fighting spirit under pressure. Churchill reveled in the role—he also unified and led a determined people.

London was still in flames Sunday morning; in the East End the docks blazed, as did the homes of the poor in the area. The dead, 309 in London and 142 in the suburbs, were civilians, not front-line soldiers. In addition, there were more than 1,300 seriously injured. Fire fighters—many volunteers—continued to try to put out the flames.

For the people of London, and eventually other English cities, the winter of the Blitz was a time of exhilaration and horror. A class-conscious people drew together to face a common enemy—and to deal with the horrendous fires, the bomb damage, and the delicate problem of delayed-action bombs or unexploded bombs. Day after day and night after night, relentlessly, the Luftwaffe came over; on September 13 the bombs damaged both St. Paul's Cathedral and Buckingham Palace. This placed Their Majesties, as it did the population of London, in the front lines.

When the Luftwaffe came over on September 15, a somewhat recovered RAF rose up to meet the bombers and their escorts for one of the most decisive battles of the Battle. British newspapers headlined that the Germans had lost 185 aircraft (of a force of more than 200 bombers and 700 fighters). In fact, the Luftwaffe lost 60 planes to the RAF's 26 fighters (half of whose pilots were saved).

If the RAF's victory was not as spectacular as claimed, it was still a victory. Added to that was the further damage done by British bombers to the invasion craft along the Belgian and French coasts. Two days later Hitler postponed Sealion "until further notice."

The Luftwaffe continued to sow human misery in London, especially by night (the British had not yet developed an efficient night-fighter system), which boomed with the sound of bombardment, the crack of British antiaircraft guns, and shrilled to the air raid sirens.

Then came another switch in Goering's strategy. Because of the heavy losses by day, the air offensive would concentrate on night operations. The night offensive began on November 14 with an attack on Coventry, noted for its beautiful cathedral—and its aircraft industry. The formation of about 450 German bombers bombed effectively in the clear moonlit night and devastated central Coventry. Other industrial cities also became targets: Bristol, Plymouth, Birmingham, Liverpool, Southampton, and others as the Blitz mounted in fury (even small elements of the Italian Air Force joined in some of the raids).

But the London blitz was not over; the year closed with an attack that did much damage to central London—the City. But British nerve did not break. A dogged, grim humor became common as the British refused to surrender. The motto became "London can take it." The spirit was not unique, as other British cities took it too.

Prime Minister Churchill, as well as the King and Queen, visited badly bombed areas with the expected results. Churchill was vehemently advised by the survivors, "Give it 'em back!" and he would. On another occasion a man shouted to King George VI, in a definite cockney dialect, "You're a great king!"

"You're a great people!" shouted the King in reply.

The British endured and the Blitz tapered off by the close of 1940, primarily because of the weather. In March of 1941 the heavy bombing began again (now to be met by British night fighters), accomplishing little but to decimate the Luftwaffe. By mid-May 1941 it could be said that the Blitz was over, partly because it had not beaten the British and primarily because Hitler had decided to break off the Battle with Britain to wage his holy war against Communism.

The Battle of Britain and the Blitz marked the opening of total war against noncombatants, which would come back to haunt the Germans with devastating fury later—also delivered from the air. During this period 40,000 British civilians died and 46,000 were injured. These casualty figures were considerably larger than those for military personnel during the same period.

During 1940 new battlefronts were opened by the blundering Mussolini, who initiated his own sideshow. The still-not-yet world war was, indeed, spilling over. It remained for Hitler to dream himself into a nightmare. On December 18, 1940, he ordered "Barbarossa," in which he said that the "German armed forces must be prepared to crush Soviet Russia in a quick campaign before the end of the war against England."

Later he would say euphorically, "When 'Barbarossa' begins, the world will hold its breath . . ."

The German Navy enjoyed its greatest successes, and its worst losses, in the German conquest of Scandinavia—particularly the invasion of Norway. The British Navy proved a tough adversary; in this photograph German minesweepers clear the waters off the coast of Norway.

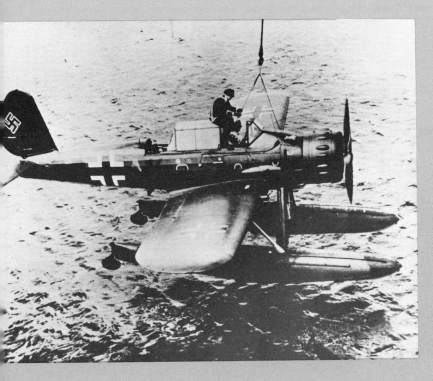

Following the conquest of Norway, the Germans established an extended system of naval and air bases out of which British shipping was severely attacked. This floatplane, an Arado 196, operated out of Norwegian bases in antisubmarine patrols.

Imperial War Museum, London

A British Royal Air Force Gladiator at Andalsnes, in central Norway, camouflaged against the Luftwaffe. This base, within easy bombing range of German aircraft, was abandoned early in June. The surviving aircraft were flown to the British carrier Glorious *for return to Britain, but the* Glorious *was sunk after an attack by the German battle cruisers* Scharnhorst *and* Gneisenau.

A German coastal gun position, Norway, in the winter of 1940. The British Royal Navy and Royal Air Force necessitated the manning of such posts.

The National Archives

The legendary Maginot Line, built in 1929–34. Protecting the eastern frontier of France from Longwy, France, to Switzerland, it was a symbol of French military attitudes during the so-called Phony War. When Hitler ended that phase of the war, German troops merely went around the line or flew over it.

Although the surrender of Norway ended systematic fighting, the Germans suffered harassment from Norwegian resistance fighters and Allied commando raids. Some 300,000 German troops were tied up in Norway for the duration of the war.

End of the Phony War, May 1940—German paratroopers drop from the skies over the Netherlands in the vicinity of The Hague and Rotterdam. Holland would fall in five days.

In another part of the world a French officer observes the training of troops in French Indochina, where trouble with the Japanese was expected. These troops appear to be equipped for the wrong war.

French soldiers preparing artillery shells for the end of the Phony War. French military thinking, like this photograph, was rooted in the Great War and not ready for blitzkrieg.

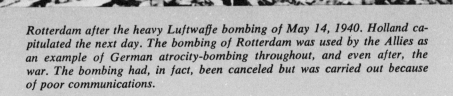

*Rotterdam after the heavy Luftwaffe bombing of May 14, 1940. Holland ca-
pitulated the next day. The bombing of Rotterdam was used by the Allies as
an example of German atrocity-bombing throughout, and even after, the
war. The bombing had, in fact, been canceled but was carried out because
of poor communications.*

Where the Dutch or the Belgians succeeded in destroying bridges, German ground troops were ready to cross with portable, inflatable rafts.

German occupation poster affording Frenchmen the opportunity to fight against Bolshevism in the Waffen SS (the fighting branch of the SS).

SI TU VEUX QUE LA FRANCE VIVE
TU COMBATTRAS DANS LA WAFFEN ⚡⚡
CONTRE LE BOLCHEVISME

"AUX ARMES CITOYENS"!..

UN SEUL COMBAT
POUR UNE SEULE PATRIE

*A French recruiting poster
calling for French unity.*

While the Allies were preoccupied with the German attack in the Lowlands, the main thrust was made through the "impassable" Ardennes into France. By June 25 all fighting ended in France. French troops surrender.

Hitler in Paris, June 1940.

French Embassy Press Division

Although there was collaboration by Frenchmen with the Germans (particularly at the demoralized top), German recruiting posters were generally ineffectual, and what the conquerors got instead was a secret army of French Resistance fighters who interfered with Nazi communications and who fought out of the darkness and the hills.

Goering (fifth from right) and his staff study the English Channel and, in the distance, the cliffs of England. Only the waters of the Channel and the English stood against Hitler's conquest of Europe. Goering and his Luftwaffe were assigned the task of solving the problem.

Imperial War Museum, London

Ready for the invasion: offshore defense installations protected the most vulnerable landing areas of Britain. The British were determined to permit no German boot on British soil.

These unimpressive structures determined the outcome of the Battle of Britain. Radar towers that detected the approach of German aircraft before they reached England— to be intercepted by the Hurricanes and Spitfires of the RAF.

First line of defense, Battle of Britain. Hawker Hurricanes, guided by radar, set out to intercept German aircraft.

A Battle of Britain control center: an operations room from which, through the employment of radar, the RAF fighters were vectored toward the approaching Luftwaffe formations.

Aftermath of a Luftwaffe attack. The industrial town of Luton, England, although it produced tanks and aircraft, was also a leading hat-manufacturing center. German bombers on this mission did not hit a tank or aircraft factory.

Over the English Channel, German He-111s with full bombloads (about 3,000 pounds each) head for English targets.

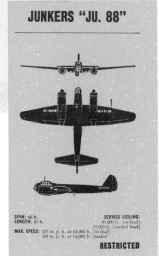

JUNKERS "JU. 88"

SPAN: 66 ft.
LENGTH: 47 ft.

SERVICE CEILING:
30,000 ft. (no load)
14,000 ft. (normal load)

MAX. SPEED: 287 m. p. h. at 14,000 ft. (no load)
269 m. p. h. at 14,000 ft. (loaded)

RESTRICTED

The wreckage of a German bomber smolders in a Kent apple orchard. The bulk of the interceptions—and air battles—occurred over the county of Kent, south of London. Spent shells, battle debris raining from the air, and jettisoned bombs gave Kent the nickname "Hell's Corner."

Fox Photos

A Luftwaffe pilot, rescued from the English Channel, arrives in Britain as a prisoner of war. He was lucky; many German pilots perished in the treacherous Channel during the Battle of Britain.

Imperial War Museum, London

Londoners seeking shelter from Luftwaffe bomber attacks in the Underground. The station stop is Elephant and Castle, in the Lambeth section of London.

London burning at the height of the Blitz in the winter of 1940.

*"This is London,"
American reporter
Edward R. Murrow
informs American radio
listeners of the progress of
the war over England.*

Unimpressive beginning of disaster:
Italian artillery and troops
moving into Egypt, September 1940.

British armor moves through an Italian minefield under artillery fire.
Though better equipped, the Italians were not as well led as the British
and proved no match for them.

As he had in Greece, Hitler had to come to the aid of fellow dictator Mussolini in North Africa, a move that would transform it into a major battleground.

Typical desert landscape and symbol of Italian fortunes in Egypt. A supply truck, destroyed by a land mine, has been pulled off the road.

1941

A World at War

O N THE LAST DAY of 1940, Adolf Hitler, in writing to his partner-in-
war Mussolini, expressed regret that Spanish dictator Franco had
chosen to stay out of the conflict. As the war progressed into the new
year, Hitler must have longed also for Mussolini's absenteeism. The Fascist dictator's vain attempts to imitate the Caesars created distractions
that turned Hitler's attentions way from his chosen battlegrounds.

Mussolini, envious of Hitler's conquests, set out unilaterally and managed to inflame the Mediterranean with an invasion of Greece (October
1940) and to stir up a desert war in Africa. Although the British appeared to be fully occupied at the time with the Battle of Britain and the
Blitz, Mussolini's meddling—to Hitler's discomfort—alerted Churchill's
interest in the Balkans and the future of the Suez Canal.

By the time Hitler dispatched his letter, it was obvious that he would
have to bail out his Axis partner, whose troops were in trouble in Greece
and Africa.

The Italian East African empire crumbled first, with Italian moves
into British Somaliland from Ethiopia, and into the Sudan from Eritrea.
Victory, temporary as it turned out, in British Somaliland denied the
British the port of Berbera on the Gulf of Aden, as well as the French
port of Djibouti in their Somaliland.

The blow against the Italians in East Africa came in February 1941,
when the British 12th African Division struggled through the northern
frontier of Kenya and into Italian Somaliland. Little immediate success
was expected because of the terrain and the threat of rainy weather, but
Italian defenses collapsed surprisingly fast (using Ethiopian troops to
delay the oncoming British was a serious Italian blunder). By mid-May
the East African campaign was over and attention could be given the
more critical battlefields in the Western Desert of Libya, North Africa.

The British were heavily outnumbered in Africa by Italian forces; in North Africa about 36,000 British, New Zealand, and Indian troops faced an Italian force of over 200,000 Italian and Italian colonial troops. The Commander in Chief of the British Middle Eastern Theatre was the dour, taciturn General Sir Archibald Wavell. His commander in the Western Desert was Lieutenant General Richard O'Connor. When Italy declared war in June of 1940, Italian troops in Libya represented a distinct threat to Egypt and the Suez Canal.

The Italian commander, Marshal Rodolfo Graziani, reluctantly under Mussolini's goading (and the threat of dismissal) began to move gingerly into Egypt along the coastal road in September. Outnumbered, the British withdrew to take a stand deeper inside Egypt. Graziani led his army some 60 miles beyond the frontier to a small collection of huts named Sidi Barrani. There he stopped and began to dig in.

While Mussolini, having tasted his first triumph of the war, demanded more, and while Graziani wavered, Wavell turned the problem over to O'Connor. As the Italians fortified Sidi Barrani and other positions in Egypt, O'Connor collected his forces—less than 35,000 men, but no less than 275 tanks. The mobility of armored vehicles and tanks would decide the battle in the desert war.

On December 9, 1940, O'Connor struck. The Royal Navy shelled Sidi Barrani from the Mediterranean, artillery fire pounded from the east, and tanks swept through and around the Italian positions. The next day Sidi Barrani fell and thousands of Italian prisoners were taken, "five acres of officers and two hundred acres of other ranks," Churchill crowed.

General Erwin Rommel, commander of the Afrika Korps and brilliant tank tactician, during the opening operations of the German offensive in Cyrenaica, March 1941. His vehicle is a Pz III converted into a commander's car, equipped with a radio.

Heinz J. Nowarra

EUROPE
1941

ARCTIC OCEAN

BARENTS SEA

ATLANTIC OCEAN

N

Petsamo

Murmansk

Archangel

SWEDEN

NORWAY

FINLAND

U.S.S.R.

MANNERHEIM

KARELIAN ISTHMUS

Helsinki

VOROSHILOV

Leningrad

EST.

ZHUKOV
MOSCOW

Oslo

Stockholm

LATVIA

LITH.

BALTIC SEA

LEEB

VOLGA R.

NORTH SEA

DENMARK

ELBE R.

Berlin

Warsaw

BOCK

POLAND

RUNDSTEDT

Kiev

DON R.

Stalingrad

TIMOSHENKO

DONETS R.

Rostov

IRELAND

ENGLAND

London

GERMANY

RHINE R.

CZECHOSLOVAKIA

DNEPER R.

CAUCASUS

Paris

FRANCE

SEINE R.

LOIRE R.

DANUBE R.

Vienna

AUSTRIA

HUNGARY

ROMANIA

Bucharest

Sevastopol

CRIMEA

BLACK SEA

BAY OF BISCAY

Vichy

SWITZ.

RHONE R.

ITALY

YUGOSLAVIA

Belgrade

DANUBE R.

BULGARIA

Sofia

Ankara

TURKEY

Madrid

Rome

ADRIATIC SEA

Taranto

ALBANIA

AEGEAN SEA

SPAIN

GREECE

Athens

Gibraltar

PANTELLERIA

Algiers

Tunis

MALTA

MEDITERRANEAN SEA

CRETE

sablanca

ALGERIA

TUNISIA

Tripoli

MAR.–MAY
ROMMEL

CYRENAICA

Benghazi

DEC.
AUCHINLECK

Beda Fomm

Tobruk *Bardia*

Alexandria

Sidi Barrani

EGYPT

MOROCCO

El Agheila

LIBYA

Pre-war Frontiers

Miles 500

0

Km. 500

palacios

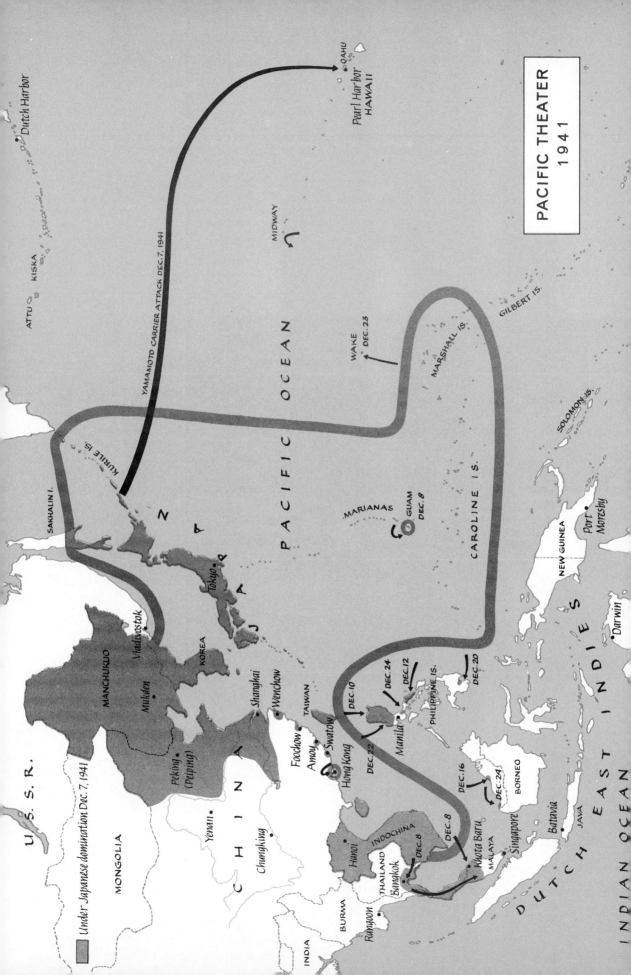

PACIFIC THEATER
1941

Dutch Harbor

ATTU   KISKA

KURILE IS.

SAKHALIN I.

MIDWAY

PACIFIC OCEAN

YAMAMOTO CARRIER ATTACK DEC. 7, 1941

OAHU
Pearl Harbor
HAWAII

WAKE
DEC. 23

GILBERT IS.

MARSHALL IS.

MARIANAS   GUAM
DEC. 8

CAROLINE IS.

SOLOMON IS.

Port
Moresby

NEW GUINEA

Darwin

J   A   P   A   N

Tokyo

Vladivostok

MANCHUKUO

Mukden

KOREA

Shanghai

Wenchow

TAIWAN

Foochow
Amoy   Swatow

Hong Kong
DEC. 22

PHILIPPINE IS.

DEC. 10   DEC. 24
DEC. 12

Manila

DEC. 20

BORNEO

DEC. 16   DEC. 24

Batavia

Java

U. S. S. R.

Under Japanese domination Dec. 7, 1941

Peking
(Peiping)

MONGOLIA

C   H   I   N   A

Yenan

Chungking

INDOCHINA
DEC. 8

Hanoi

THAILAND
Bangkok

DEC. 8

Kota Baru
MALAYA

Singapore

DUTCH   EAST   INDIES

BURMA

Rangoon

INDIA

INDIAN OCEAN

Not all of the fighting in the Mediterranean took place in the desert. Other key spots were such islands as Crete and Malta, which required supplies and weapons. Making a delivery of aircraft to Malta, strategically positioned between Tripoli and Sicily, the British aircraft carrier Ark Royal was caught by German submarine U-81 and hit by torpedoes off Gibraltar and was sunk. The crew is leaving the ship. At the end of the flight deck are several Fairey Swordfish torpedo bombers (with wings folded for storage) about to slip into the sea.

The British employment of tanks completely threw the Italians off balance. Among O'Connor's troops was the 7th Armoured Division, elements of which would become celebrated as the fast-moving, hard-hitting "Desert Rats." Their hit-and-run tactics, frequently from behind, by sweeping around and coming at the Italian positions from the rear or flank, created disorder and much confusion.

Once he had the Italians on the run, O'Connor kept them running. By January 4, 1941, when the Australians swept into Bardia in their dusty Matilda tanks, the Italians had been pushed out of Egypt. O'Connor did not stop there but continued into Libya, sending the 6th Australian Division in pursuit of the Italian army through Cyrenaica (the northern bulge of Libya), along the coastal road that Mussolini had built, and dispatched the Desert Rats southwestward, through the desert, to cut off the retreat.

The British reached the coast at Beda Fomm before the Italians; after a handful of British tanks put most of the Italian tanks out of the battle, Italian troops surrendered in droves. It was the end of the Italian Tenth Army. Some 3,000 British troops took 20,000 prisoners at Beda Fomm.

On February 6, Adolf Hitler summoned a young tank commander who had distinguished himself in the French campaign. He was Major General Erwin Rommel and was given command of two divisions, one of panzers, which would come to be known as the Afrika Korps. Hitler had decided he would remedy the situation Mussolini had caused in

North Africa. On February 12, 1941—with O'Connor ordered to stop his advance into Libya—the man the British would respectfully, with no little admiration, call "The Desert Fox," was flown into Tripoli, which had been the objective that O'Connor never got to take. The desert war was about to take a new turn.

Rommel, technically subordinate to Italian commander General Italo Gariboldi, quickly revealed himself as a man with a strong character; imaginative and with a grasp of what should be done about the situation in North Africa.

Wavell did not expect the Afrika Korps to be ready to launch an offensive in the Western Desert before May. But by early March there were small clashes in the El Agheila area, in Libya on the border between Tripolitania and Cyrenaica. Then on March 24 a heavy raid by Axis troops occupied El Agheila, and Rommel, taking advantage of the situation (the British positions were lightly manned and poorly equipped), pushed deeper into Cyrenaica: the place names of O'Connor's victories were then reversed as Rommel deployed his armored forces and pushed the British troops across the top of Cyrenaica back toward Egypt. On April 4, the important port of Benghazi fell; on the seventh, to the deep chagrin of the British High Command, several general officers fell into the hands of German reconnaissance patrols.

By April 15, Axis troops were back inside Egypt, having by-passed the surrounded, British-held fort at Tobruk, almost at the position where O'Connor had begun his offensive against the Italians four months before. Rommel had canceled that out in a month.

The thorn in his side was besieged Tobruk, defended by Australian infantry and armor; his supply lines were stretched—always a problem to be considered in the desert. Rommel's rapid advance had disturbed his Italian superiors, as it did the German High Command, whose Chief of Staff, General Franz Halder, dispatched an aide to Africa in order "to head off this soldier gone stark mad."

Except that Rommel had brought them closer to the Suez Canal than they had ever been before. Wavell buffered the defenses on the Libyan-Egyptian frontier with what troops he could, and Rommel's spectacular offensive ran out of momentum. The stalemate ended the second phase of what would become a strange, oscillating, to-and-fro war.

Aroused, Churchill ordered tank-carrying vessels to rush to Africa through the dangerous waters of the Mediterranean (where the Italian Air Force had been reinforced by units of the Luftwaffe) rather than the safer, circuitous, and longer route around the Cape of Good Hope. On May 12 a convoy reached Egypt with a cargo of tanks and fighter planes. A plan was hurried into operation and on June 12 was launched. The objective of "Battleaxe" was to drive Rommel's forces back across Cyrenaica and to relieve the troops in Tobruk. There were initial successes, but within two days it was obvious that Battleaxe, too hastily mounted with inexperienced troops, had failed. Rommel's tired, though hardened, veterans in their well-prepared positions stood their ground and then counterattacked.

Stalemate again and, so far as Churchill was concerned, the end of Wavell. He was replaced by General Sir Claude Auchinleck as Commander in Chief, Middle East, in July. The summer of 1941 passed in the Western Desert with little change on either side. What had been known as the Western Desert Force was renamed the Eighth Army and placed under the command of General Sir Alan Cunningham.

Cunningham, with reinforcements and an influx of supplies and armor, began his offensive on November 18 ("Operation Crusader"), which failed in its first objective, the relief of Tobruk, and suffered heavy tank losses primarily because the Germans had more powerful antitank weapons, if not a preponderance of tanks. Auchinleck relieved Cunningham and replaced him with Major General Neil M. Ritchie, and Crusader was resumed on December 5. On December 10, Tobruk was cleared of its Axis siege and Ritchie and the Eighth Army shoved the Afrika Korps and the Italians back across Cyrenaica until, on December 24, they occupied Benghazi.

While the British were successful in Crusader, they had suffered heavy loss of armor; troop casualties were heavy also, although Axis losses

Mussolini, having stirred up the Balkans and the Mediterranean, placed Hitler in an embarrassing position at a time when he would have preferred to concentrate on his archenemy, Russia. To place a strong German force on strategic Crete, Hitler ordered the island taken by German troops. Supplies for this venture are being loaded into a Ju-52 in North Africa.

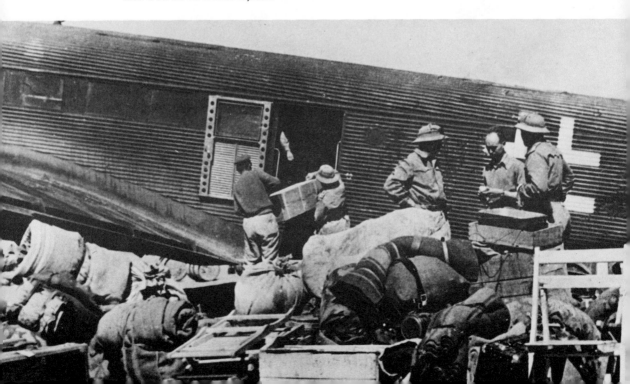

(33,000) were almost double that of the British (under 18,000). Most of the Axis loss consisted of Italian troops, and the bulk of the Germans captured were administrative rather than battle troops. British losses were difficult-to-replace veterans.

By the end of 1941, what with the surprises from a new Eastern Front and the Pacific, Mussolini's chosen area for conquest went into eclipse, so far as the world's attention was concerned. His move into the Balkans disturbed Hitler, for, should the British gain a foothold there on the pretense of aiding the Greeks, then the RAF would be within bombing range of the Ploesti Rumanian oil fields and might complicate his Operation Barbarossa. Hitler sewed up Rumania and Hungary in 1940, both nations joining the Axis; in March 1941, Bulgaria and Yugoslavia were "invited" to join and accepted. Yugoslav rebels objected and overthrew the government to form an anti-Nazi regime. Hitler's reply was "Operation Punishment" (April 1941), which mercilessly annihilated the opposition. Belgrade was bombed for three days until it became little more than rubble and 17,000 died. By April 17, except for those who took refuge in the hills, Yugoslavia became a member of the Axis.

Within a week, Greece, which had proved to be too much for Mussolini's forces, also surrendered to the Nazis. The British forces, air and ground, that had been sent there the previous November were evacuated by the Royal Navy by April 29—a minor Dunkirk.

The island of Crete, strategically positioned in the eastern Mediterranean, was the next objective. Crete was defended by Greek troops that

A Ju-52 burns after being hit by antiaircraft fire as German paratroopers descend onto the island of Crete. Though successful, the Crete operation soured Hitler on future airborne ventures.

Imperial War Museum, London

On the eve of "Barbarossa," the Nazi assault on Soviet Russia, Hitler and Rundstedt, commander of Army Group South for the invasion.

had been evacuated from the mainland and British forces (New Zealanders) under the command of Major General Bernard Freyberg. Although the Royal Navy interfered with German convoys, it was General Kurt Student's airborne troops, with the aid of the Luftwaffe, that took Crete. Once Maleme airport was in German hands (at great cost to the Germans), reinforcements and equipment poured into Crete.

After almost a week of bombing, the airborne invasion began on May 20—by the end of the month yet another British evacuation was under way. The Germans had secured another victory, but at a great price. Of the 22,000 German troops that had been employed in "Operation Mercure," nearly a third were killed or wounded. The greatest Nazi airborne operation of the war resulted in the elimination of such future German operations.

But with the Balkans under his heel and with the Luftwaffe in control of most of the Mediterranean (since the British had audaciously crippled the Italian fleet with carrier aircraft in its own home base at Taranto the previous November), with that "madman" Rommel teaching the British and the Italians a thing or two in North Africa, and Churchill and the English contained in their island, Hitler could turn to his labor of love—and his major blunder of the war—Barbarossa.

"I have decided again today," Hitler said over the German radio on June 22, 1941, "to place the fate and future of the Reich and our people in the hands of our soldiers."

Barbarossa began as a classic blitzkrieg with classic results. Before dawn an artillery barrage announced the beginning; the Stukas followed. Three great German army groups, with panzers in the vanguard, plunged across the Russian frontier. Army Group North (Field Marshal Wilhelm von Leeb) moved in from East Prussia and into the Baltic states with Leningrad as the first major objective. In the sector below Army Group Center, Field Marshal Fedor von Bock was assigned to take Smolensk—and beyond that, Moscow. Army Group South (Field Marshal Karl von Rundstedt), moving in from Rumania and Hungary, was to take and occupy the western Ukraine, the great Russian indus-

83

Blitzkrieg East: He-111 bombers, heading for Russian targets, pass over German columns of the invading ground forces.

trial center, and then proceed to Kiev. The German army groups ranged along a battlefront of nearly a thousand miles, from the Black Sea to the Baltic.

Despite numerous advance warnings—from Churchill, various foreign embassies, including Washington—Stalin appeared not to take the possibility of an impending German attack seriously (the British Ambassador in Moscow even predicted the correct date). Stalin chose to place his faith in his German brother dictator and to distrust the alarums of the democracies.

Barbarossa was also a blunder by Stalin.

When the blitzkrieg suddenly erupted, one Russian commander revealed its impact in a message which read: "We are being fired upon; what shall we do?"

The Germans literally poured over the Russian positions as the unprepared Soviets fell back or were encircled and destroyed wholesale. Before June 22 ended, some German units had pierced nearly fifty miles into Russia. Behind the lines, German dive bombers struck Russian airfields along the entire front (over 60 bases) and, according to some estimates, more than 2,000 Russian fighter aircraft were destroyed

Army Group North moved through the Baltic countries from East Prussia toward Leningrad. A panzer unit is bogged down in a Lithuanian field. Even so, the conquest of the Baltic states proceeded rapidly and German troops were welcomed as liberators initially—and then the SS took over.

A German antitank gun crew watches a Russian village burn under Stalin's "scorched earth" policy.

As the infantry moves forward, a German antiaircraft crew scans the sky for Russian planes, which were all but nonexistent in the summer of 1941.

Preparing for the German advance on their city, citizens of Leningrad dig in and build fortifications during the late summer of 1941. Nearly a million people of all occupations, children, men, as well as women, participated. This defense line is being constructed on the Neva River, which the Germans reached but never succeeded in crossing.

within the first two days. Prisoners were taken by the hundreds of thousands. Few military authorities believed the war would last through the summer.

The Red Army, reeling, fell back or was swallowed by the seemingly invincible Wehrmacht. As the Germans continued to move on three fronts, Stalin broadcast a plan of action to the Russian people. He defined the war as a "People's War," not merely a war involving the Red Army. He warned of the consequences of defeat—and the SS willingly proved him right—and called for "a scorched earth."

Stalin also ordered all farmers to leave nothing behind, livestock, grain, equipment—what could not be removed to the rear must be destroyed. Entire factories were dismantled, moved, and back in production deep inside Russia within weeks under this plan.

The Wehrmacht was to encounter an implacable enemy—stubborn, resourceful, and willing to die for Mother Russia in Stalin's "Great Patriotic War" (it is not known as World War II in the Soviet Union). In his speech made in early July, Stalin also promised his people aid from the democracies, Churchill having pledged whatever help Britain could spare and Roosevelt American assistance "short of war."

But there were also the problems associated with the initial victories: the deeper the Germans drove into Russia, the more space their troops had to occupy and the longer the supply lines stretched. Maps were not the sole concern of the German commanders—so was the calendar. In order to fulfill Barbarossa all three of the army groups would have to plunge ahead speedily: beyond Leningrad in the north to Archangel, past Moscow in the center, and to the Volga in the south. This would have to be accomplished before the dreaded Russian winter set in.

Early in July it appeared that Germany had acquired a new ally when the Finns (who had declared war on Russia on June 26), led by Mannerheim, struck out across the Karelian Isthmus. This suited Hitler well, for he visualized two armies, his and Mannerheim's, closing in on Leningrad. But Mannerheim's plan did not include conquest, nor an alliance with Hitler. Once he had taken back what the Russians had seized from Finland, he refused to co-operate with the Germans. Leningrad would have to be left to Leeb's Army Group North. In the center, by July 16, Smolensk had fallen to the Germans. Guderian's panzer forces were then taken from Army Group Center to assist Army Group South's advance on Kiev, where, by September, the Soviet Army would lose half a million men.

Hitler was not happy, however. During a brief lull in August, when plans for a continuation of the Russian war were projected by his general staff, Hitler informed them that what they had in mind was "not in line with my intentions." The generals had proposed to continue on to Moscow, but Hitler chose to set aside his earlier wish to concentrate on the Crimea, the industrial Donets River Basin and the Caucasus, and its oil, in the south. The bulk of Army Group North's armor would be drawn off; the siege of Leningrad, which would be encircled but not taken, was left to the infantry.

Hitler's decision stunned his generals. And then on September 6, Hitler changed his mind again. Moscow became the major objective.

Hitler's erratic, grandiose military schemes—while shockingly successful initially—placed heavy, and often impossible, loads upon the German military machine. Hitler was not the only factor, of course. The fighting Russian—male and female—not only proved to be expendable in what appeared to be unlimited numbers, but fought fanatically. The vastness of Russia was a factor and, when the impetus of the German blitzkrieg slowed down and time passed, there was the Russian winter.

And in 1941 Russia had the earliest—and coldest—winter in a half century.

Dispatches from Russia continued to bring the news of German victories as Stalingrad was cut off from the rest of Russia, as the battle for Kiev ended and the battle for Moscow began. By October 12 women and children were being evacuated from the capital, and four days later the government followed. Martial law was proclaimed, and Stalin, who had chosen to remain in Moscow, placed Marshal Georgi Zhukov in command of the armies defending Moscow.

The Wehrmacht enters Aleksandriya, to the south and beyond Kiev; these are an advance guard of Rundstedt's Army Group South.

Kiev under siege; by September it was encircled and its garrison captured or killed in great numbers—so were tens of thousands of Jews in a nearby ravine, Babi Yar.

The German advance had been slowed by the autumn rains and the relentless sniping of guerrilla fighters behind the lines. In November, when the freezing weather struck, tanks were literally frozen in their tracks. But by late November the Wehrmacht was within miles of Moscow. Zhukov, holding his best troops in reserve, stalled the Germans by feeding the ill-trained, poorly equipped civilian home guard into the battle to be slaughtered. Exhausted, the Germans hoped for Hitler's permission to halt, dig in, and wait for spring. But the Fuehrer would not hear of it.

Then on the morning of December 6, Zhukov struck back, drawing upon some twenty-five fresh divisions. Army Group Center reeled under the smashing attack; the blitzkrieg was over. Unable to dig into the frozen earth the tired Germans had no prepared positions to fall back to and the German lines broke.

While Americans kept a wary eye on the war in Europe, hoping to keep out of it, there were stirrings in the mysterious Far East. In Japan militarists in the government urged an alliance with the Axis and the seizure of Indochina. Aloof from the turmoil was Emperor Hirohito, "Imperial Son of Heaven of Great Japan," seen presiding over a meeting of the Japanese Diet, where demands for Japanese expansion were voiced; these voices were ignored in the United States.

The National Archives

Ill-equipped for the Russian winter, German soldiers suffered mechanical breakdowns by trucks and tanks. Because it was thought that Barbarossa would be successfully concluded before winter, the German troops had no winter clothing—countless numbers froze to death, some at their posts.

The same was not true for Hitler's unhappy High Command. When he and his Commander in Chief of the Army, Brauchitsch, differed, the latter asked to be relieved of his command because of "illness." Commander of Army Group South, Rundstedt, was relieved when he permitted his exhausted troops to fall back in the face of the heavy Russian attacks. Leeb, of Army Group North, had suggested a withdrawal from the Stalingrad front and was immediately relieved of his command. Bock, Army Group Center, soon joined Brauchitsch on the "sick" list and went home. Guderian, the panzer virtuoso, who frequently regarded Hitler as a military ninny and who disregarded his Fuehrer's orders and let his nearly exhausted troops draw back, soon joined the others. It appeared that the only retreat from the Russian Front was carried out by the Officer Corps.

The ordinary German soldier had to remain, however, facing an implacable, even merciless, Soviet fighting man—and an even more ruthless Russian winter.

90

The ultimate irony occurred around Christmas time. Hitler assumed command of the Wehrmacht.

On Christmas Day, 1941, it might be noted, in beleaguered Leningrad, 4,000 people died of starvation.

The precipitate and highly successful Japanese attack on Pearl Harbor was no spur-of-the-moment military adventure. Diplomatic relations between Japan and the United States had deteriorated since the early Thirties, and the various trade restrictions enforced by the United States (of especial importance was an embargo on oil and steel) aggravated the situation. Japanese military adventures in the Far East further aroused American concern. The American Pacific Fleet moved from its berth in California to Pearl Harbor in Hawaii.

While Japanese envoys and American diplomats discussed peace in Washington, D.C., Japanese military leaders discussed war in Tokyo. Since mid-October of 1941, when Army General Hideki Tojo was appointed Prime Minister of Japan, a military clique dominated international policy.

On November 26, on the day an official demand came from the United States that Japan withdraw from China, a day when German panzers lay within twenty-five miles of Moscow, a large Japanese carrier force moved out of its bases in the Kurile Islands and slipped into the Northern Pacific.

Despite several warnings, including the reading of intercepted Japanese coded messages, the Americans were not prepared for what oc-

A Japanese delegation pays honor to Hitler, cementing the Tripartite Pact; Japanese military leaders, certain that Hitler would engage the West, were preparing to move in the Far East.

curred at Pearl Harbor on Sunday morning, December 7, 1941. Some 200 miles north of Hawaii the first Japanese aircraft began taking off the six carriers: dive bombers ("Vals"), torpedo bombers ("Kates"), level bombers, and a deadly aircraft unknown to the Americans, the Zero fighter. Sweeping over in two waves, the bombers concentrated on the eight big ships of the American Pacific Fleet at anchor in Battleship Row around Ford Island in Pearl Harbor. Simultaneously, attacks were made on Navy, Marine, and Army airfields on Oahu. In less than two hours, as the last of the attackers returned to their carriers, Pearl Harbor —and the Pacific Fleet—had become a shambles.

In exchange for about a hundred men, five midget submarines, and twenty-nine aircraft, the Japanese had left behind 2,280 dead or missing Americans, with an additional thousand wounded. The fleet was seriously crippled; American air power in the Pacific was minimal.

The Japanese enjoyed a stunning victory, the brainchild of Admiral Isoroku Yamamoto, Commander in Chief of the Combined Japanese Fleet. An advocate of air power, Yamamoto was also aware of the dangers of an aroused America (where he had spent several years) and its war-making potential. Unless the Japanese victory were sudden, swift, and thorough, Yamamoto warned, Japan could only look forward to inevitable defeat.

The National Archives

To iron out diplomatic differences between Japan and the United States, Ambassador Kichisaburo Nomura (onetime ambassador to Germany) and Special Envoy Saburo Kurusu were dispatched to Washington to discuss the problems. They were unaware of plans for a Japanese surprise attack in the Pacific. This photograph, taken during the period of negotiations with Secretary of State Cordell Hull, was widely circulated later as a propoganda shot revealing wily Japanese duplicity. Nomura and Kurusu were as stunned as Hull by the events that occurred at Pearl Harbor.

Japanese photo of Ford Island—"Battleship Row" in Pearl Harbor
under attack by dive bombers. In the foreground the Utah (second
from right) lists after torpedoing. On the far side of the island a geyser
of water splashes up as the Japanese attacker banks away.

Naval Air Station, Pearl Harbor, after bombing
and strafing by Japanese planes.

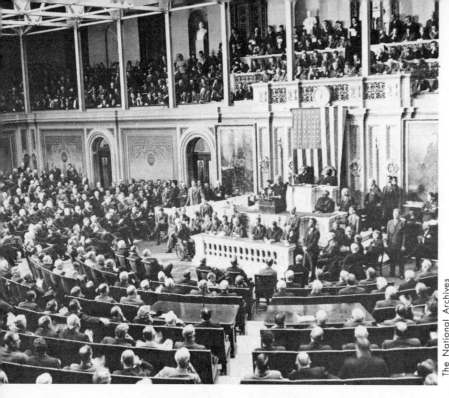

Monday, December 8, 1941, President Franklin D. Roosevelt delivers his "Day of Infamy" speech to Congress asking for a declaration of war on Japan.

But as the victorious Japanese formations flew back to their carriers, Commander Mitsuo Fuchida, the over-all leader of the bombings, was troubled by one gnawing realization: there had not been one American aircraft carrier at Pearl Harbor. It was a hauntingly ominous thought.

Another omission was the oil storage facilities in the Navy Yard at Pearl Harbor, containing nearly 10,000,000 barrels of fuel oil. These and the submarine base were practically untouched by the otherwise thorough Japanese attackers. The carriers, the submarines, and the oil would play critical roles in future Pacific fighting, to the heavy cost of the Japanese. But on the afternoon of December 7, 1941, to all the world it appeared as if the Japanese had indeed carried out a brilliant, even decisive, military masterstroke—and they had.

President Franklin D. Roosevelt made his "Day of Infamy" speech to Congress and the nation the next day, asking for a declaration of war (he made one slip: referring at one point to "Germany's air squadrons" bombing Oahu), and was overwhelmingly backed by Congress.

True to his word, Winston Churchill declared war on Japan, even before Congress had voted for war. Roosevelt, although his slip revealed a concern with Germany, did not ask for a declaration of war on Germany (although both he and Churchill agreed that Nazi Germany was the greater threat). Hitler filled the gap. On December 11, 1941, he declared war on the United States.

With fighting raging in Russia, Africa, over nighttime Britain, in the Atlantic, in the Pacific—with a series of Japanese invasions in Malaya, Hong Kong, the Philippines—the world, for the first time in history, was truly at war.

94

Jarrett Collection

Units of the Afrika Korps unloading at a North African port; in the foreground on the dock are two Pz IIIs (Panzerkampfwagen), a more formidable adversary than the Italian tanks the British had fought against in Egypt.

Desert warriors: Lieutenant General Richard O'Connor, commander of British forces in the Western Desert, and his chief, General Sir Archibald Wavell. O'Connor's handling of the campaign, and his defeat of Italian troops, brought unwelcome aid from Hitler.

One of the most respected and dreaded guns of the war: a German 88-millimeter, used against both tanks and aircraft. This one is mounted on a mobile chassis for the rapid movement of desert warfare.

A Junker Ju-52 stirs up the sand of Tripoli. The Ju-52 served primarily as a transport aircraft, although it could be used as a bomber. Its slowness made it an easy prey to enemy fighters, but its efficiency as a carrier of supplies and men was excellent. Pilots affectionately called the all-metal craft "Iron Annie."

Just as he stumbled into North Africa, Mussolini did the same in the Balkans, enkindling that traditionally incendiary area with his invasions of Greece and Yugoslavia. In this photo troops of the Italian cavalry move along a road at Brod, Yugoslavia. As before, Hitler would have to come to Mussolini's rescue.

Panzers, in co-ordination with the Luftwaffe, speed into Russia, June 22, 1941. The Soviets were so taken unawares that as supplies from Russia for Germany crossed the frontier from one direction, invading German units came from the other.

Not all of Barbarossa was lightning warfare. Horse-drawn artillery was part of the strength of the Wehrmacht. In June, Russian roads were dust; when the rains came they turned to viscous muck.

"The maps we were given were all wrong," Rundstedt wrote of the Russian invasion. *"The roads that had been marked nice and red and thick on a map turned out to be tracks . . . Even railroads which were to be used by us simply did not exist . . . I realized soon after the attack had begun that everything that had been written about Russia was nonsense."*

In a carefully posed photo a Lithuanian farm girl welcomes panzer troops.

If not thoroughly prepared for Russian roads, the invading Germans were ready for the rivers and streams with rafts, powered boats, or, as here, amphibious vehicles.

Smolensk, in the path of Army Group Center's drive for Moscow, burns under artillery and aerial bombardment.

Initial Russian casualties of Barbarossa were high partly because of poor leadership and partly because of inferior equipment. A Russian armored car, its crew killed, burns in the wake of the panzers.

German panzers advance on Smolensk, where by early August more than 100,000 Russian prisoners were taken.

Seemingly unstoppable, a German panzer moves forward past yet another burning Russian village.

Russian captives, herded by a single German soldier, are led into the nightmare of the Nazi SS treatment of the Untermensch *(subhumans), Jews and Russians. By September the Germans had taken more than 500,000 prisoners.*

Like Russian armor, Russian aircraft in the early phase of Barbarossa were no match for German equipment. This Polikarpov I-16 (also known as "Rata," or Rat) was a veteran of the Spanish Civil War, where it was proved inferior to the Me-109.

Despite the lack of rail resources in Russia, the Germans also employed heavy artillery in their siege of the larger cities.

Russian civilians, probably partisans who attempted to hold up the German advance, were shot on capture. Nazi treatment of the Russian civilian population was brutal, resulting in the death of about ten million.

Colonel General Heinz Guderian, commander of the 2nd Armored Division of Army Group Center, was one of Germany's most effective tank commanders. He spearheaded the drive to Moscow—and came within 40 miles of it.

Before the autumn rains, a panzer unit easily fords a Russian stream.

Stukas take out a couple of bridges near Novgorod, a tactic that would cut off supplies to beleaguered Leningrad.

The Ju-87 Stuka, after its abject failure in the Battle of Britain, made a temporary comeback during the early Russian campaign. It proved effective in pinpoint dive bombing as a tank destroyer.

Horses were more efficient on certain roads than heavy tanks; a German gun crew moves into position.

Tank tracks of the German advance before the autumn rains; the churned-up powder manufactured by tread would become a natural tank trap when rain-soaked.

An antitank team in a Russian field. In the foreground, the kneeling soldier carries a flame-thrower. Behind him another shoulders a bazooka-like antitank gun.

Guderian's panzers race toward Moscow; Russian light tanks are not capable of stopping them.

In the path of war: a Russian woman watches her home go up in smoke.

With the coming of the dreaded Russian winter, Hitler had lost his Barbarossa gamble. A German soldier is tossed out of his motorcycle after a skid in the snow. This was mild compared to what would follow for the Wehrmacht in wintry Russia.

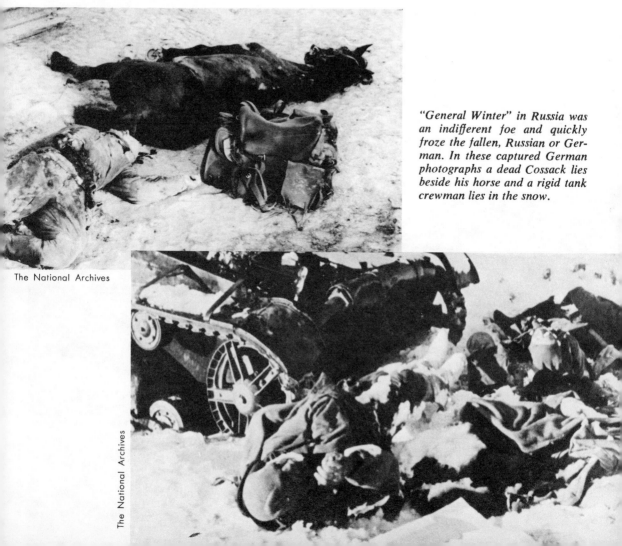

"General Winter" in Russia was an indifferent foe and quickly froze the fallen, Russian or German. In these captured German photographs a dead Cossack lies beside his horse and a rigid tank crewman lies in the snow.

General Hideki Tojo, who replaced the peace-seeking Prince Fumimaro Konoye as Premier of Japan. The leader of the military faction inside the Japanese Government, Tojo was determined to establish a "New Order" in Asia, which would open with an attack on the United States.

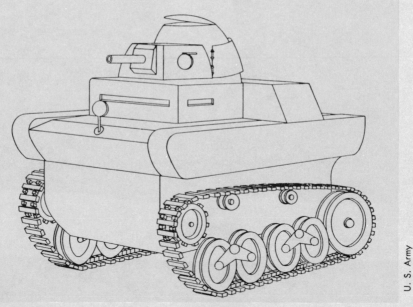

1. Crew: 3 men.
2. Armament: 1 37-mm gun, 1 light machine gun.
3. Ammunition:
4. Armor, thickness:
   Upper structure: 0.75 to 1.0 inch.
   Front: 0.5 to 0.75 inch.
   Sides:
5. Turret: Hand traverse.
6. Vision: Probably indirect for driver.
7. Ventilation:
8. Communications:
9. Dimensions:
   Length: 16 feet.
   Width: 7 feet.
   Height: 7 feet.
10. Weight: 7 to 9 tons.
11. Motor:
    Type:
    Cooling system:
    Horsepower:
    Horsepower per ton: 7.8.

12. Drive:
13. Speed:
    Cross-country:
    Road:
    Maximum:
14. Cruising radius, at .... speed .... miles.
15. Operating distance without refill.
16. Gear speeds and ratios:
17. Turning radius:
18. Suspension type: Trailing idler.
19. Performance:
    Ground clearance:
    Climbs:
    Negotiates:
    Crosses:
    Fords:
20. Remarks: Amphibian tanks are apparently built in two sizes, one about 7 to 9 tons in weight, and one estimated to be 4 or 5 tons.

Japanese amphibian tank used from 1941 onward.

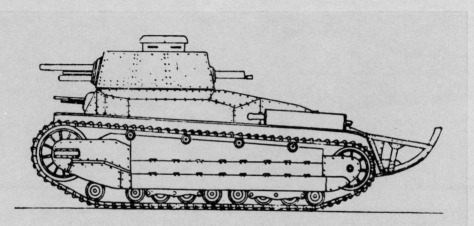

Japanese medium tank type M2594 (built 1934) used extensively from 1941.

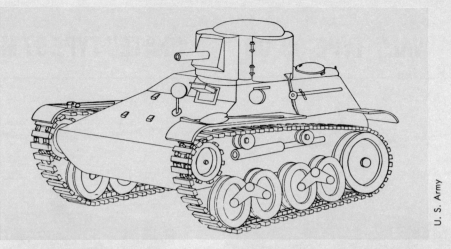

1. Crew: 2 men (1 driver, 1 gunner).
2. Armament: 1 machine gun in turret.
3. Ammunition:
4. Armor, thickness:
    Upper structure: Turret 0.75 inch.
    Front: 0.39 to 0.75 inch.
    Sides:
5. Turret: Hand traverse.
6. Vision:
    Indirect for driver.
    Slit vision for commander.
7. Ventilation:
8. Communications:
9. Dimensions:
    Length: 12 feet.
    Width: 5 feet 6 inches.
    Height: 5 feet 6 inches.
10. Weight: 4½ to 5½ tons.
11. Motor:
    Type:
    Cooling:
    Horsepower:
    Horsepower per ton.

12. Steering, brake or controlled differential:
    Brake or clutch.
13. Speed:
    Cross-country:
    Road:
    Maximum:
14. Cruising radius, at . . . . speed
    . . . . miles.
15. Operating distance without refill:
16. Gear speeds and ratios:
17. Turning radius:
18. Suspension, type: 4 bogie wheels (2 bogies) and trailing idler. Front drive.
19. Performance:
    Ground clearance:
    Climbs:
    Negotiates:
    Crosses:
    Fords:
20. Remarks: Characteristics are similar to Japanese light tanks which MacArthur reported the Japanese to be using in the Philippines.

Ishikawajima tankette M2598 (1938) (improved model observed in Japan in 1941).

Architect of the "Hawaii Operation," the surprise attack on Pearl Harbor, Admiral Isoroku Yamamoto (who, in fact, opposed a war with the United States). Yamamoto directed the attack from his flagship at the naval base at Hiroshima.

"VAL" TYPE 99 DB

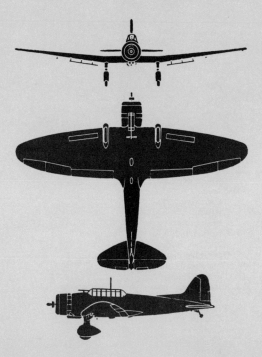

SPAN: 47 ft. 7 in.
LENGTH: 32 ft. 10 in.
APPROX. SPEED: 220 m. p. h. at 7,500 ft.

SERVICE CEILING.
27,000 ft.

RESTRICTED

"KATE" TYPE 97 MK.3 TB

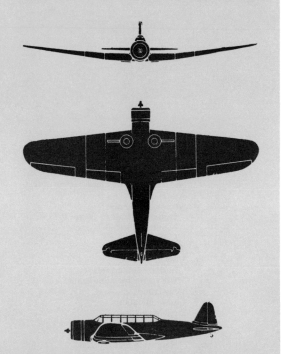

SPAN: 52 ft.
LENGTH: 34 ft.
APPROX. SPEED: 225 m. p. h. at 8,000 ft.

SERVICE CEILING:
27,500 ft

RESTRICTED

December 7, 1941: a Mitsubishi Type "O" (Zero) fighter plane leaves the deck of a carrier to escort Japanese bombers to Pearl Harbor.

Japan joins the Axis: an Italian propaganda postcard depicting a powerful Japan dealing with the American fleet.

The shambles of Wheeler Field, an Army fighter base about ten miles north of Pearl Harbor.

The destroyer Shaw *blows up in its drydock on the mainland just south of Ford Island. By this time most of the attackers had begun returning to their carriers.*

Black Christmas: General Masaharu Homma, commander of the Japanese Fourteenth Army, comes ashore in the Lingayen Gulf, Luzon, on Christmas Eve 1941. Homma would direct the conquest of the Philippines.

1942
Year of Struggle and Peril

S OME YEARS after the event Churchill revealed his reaction to the news that the United States had been forced into the war. "Being saturated and satiated with emotion and sensation," he wrote, "I went to bed and slept the sleep of the saved and the thankful." Although the United States had gradually become more overt in its aid to Britain as well as Russia, culminating in the passage of the Lend-Lease Bill in March of 1941, "neutrality" had been the American keynote. The bill empowered Roosevelt to place into the hands of Britain, by whatever convenient means, "any defense article" that might, in turn, contribute to "defense of the United States."

Churchill's post-Pearl Harbor euphoria was based upon a statement by Sir Edward Grey (who had served as British Foreign Minister during World War I). Grey likened the United States to a "great boiler. Once the fire is lighted under it, there is no limit to the power it can generate." He was, of course, referring to the industrial potential of the United States.

FDR did not share the optimism and solemnly began 1942 by declaring January 1 as a day of prayer. The days since December 7 had not been good. Japan's expansion of its so-called Greater East Asia Co-Prosperity Sphere seemed unremitting. This sphere, whose aim was really the prosperity of Japan, was planned to establish a strong line of defense running from Japan's Kurile Islands in the Northern Pacific and then southward to the Gilbert Islands, westward through the Solomons and northern New Guinea (just brushing Australia), and continuing northwestward to contain the East Indies as far as Burma. The great defense perimeter was to discourage Great Britain and the United States from interfering with the grand design, which was primarily to extract the riches, the raw materials of industry (and war) from the Southern

Regions—the real goal of Japan's attack on Pearl Harbor: the Philippines, Java, Sumatra, Malaya, Thailand.

The plan was to contain the United States by crippling its fleet at Pearl Harbor, not—as Churchill was certain it would—to light up the boiler. After the dismay and anger came unity. Historians can now see 1942 as the year in which the outcome of the war was decided, although only an optimistic warrior like Churchill, conceding it would be "a year of struggle and peril," could have imagined that. But even bolstered by a whiskey-and-soda, he was realist enough to realize the year ahead would be a hard one. The Japanese appeared to be invincible in their run of conquest. Rommel had begun moving around in North Africa and, although the Germans had been stopped in Russia, Hitler himself was promising the annihilation of the Red Army by March.

There was a greater promise for struggle and peril than victory in the new year. By January 28 Rommel had retaken Benghazi in Cyrenaica; on the same day the U. S. Eighth Air Force was activated in Georgia. On January 30, British forces were pushed by the Japanese into Singapore, and by February 4 the invaders were demanding an unconditional surrender of the island; on the same day, in another part of the world, Rommel's forces entered Derna. On February 7, Lieutenant General Sir Arthur Percival announced that Singapore would be "held to the last man." A week later more than 70,000 British and Australian troops surrendered to the last man, overwhelmed by Japanese forces.

By February 22, when it was obvious that the Philippines could not hold out, General Douglas MacArthur was ordered by Roosevelt to

The fall of Singapore, symbol of Britain's Far Eastern strength, on February 15, 1942.

EUROPE 1942

ARCTIC OCEAN

BARENTS SEA

CONVOYS

Petsamo • • Murmansk

• Archangel

U.S.S.R.

ATLANTIC OCEAN

CONVOYS

SWEDEN

FINLAND

NORWAY

MANNERHEIM

Oslo •

KARELIAN ISTHMUS

VOROSHILOV

VOLGA R.

Stockholm •

Helsinki •

Leningrad

KUECHLER

EST.

ZHUKOV
MOSCOW

ROKOSSOVSKI

CHUIKOV

NORTH SEA

BALTIC SEA

LATVIA

Tula

PAULUS'
6TH ARMY

Stalingrad

EREMENKO

DENMARK

LITH.

BOCK

DON R.

ENGLAND

ELBE R. Berlin •

Warsaw

VISTULA R.

DNEPER R.

LIST

DONETS R.

London •

Cologne •

GERMANY

POLAND

OYS

Dieppe
Rouen

Bruneval
St. Nazaire

Paris •

RHINE R.

SEINE R.

CZECHOSLOVAKIA

CAUCASUS

CRIMEA

Sevastopol •

LOIRE R.

DANUBE R.

Vienna •

AUSTRIA HUNGARY

ROMANIA

BLACK SEA

Vichy •
FRANCE

SWITZ.

RHÔNE R.

BAY OF
BISCAY

ITALY

YUGOSLAVIA

BULGARIA

DANUBE R.

TURKEY

Madrid •

CORSICA

• Rome

ADRIATIC
SEA

ALBANIA

AEGEAN
SEA

GREECE

SPAIN

SARDINIA

CRETE

TORCH

Medjez-el-Bab

SICILY

Algiers • Tunis

PANTELLERIA

MEDITERRANEAN SEA

Alexandria
El Alamein

• Gibraltar TORCH

TORCH

MALTA

Derna Tobruk ROMMEL

Oran •

Benghazi CYRENAICA

MONTGOMERY

ablanca
MOROCCO

ALGERIA

TUNISIA

Tripoli

Buerat-el-Hsur

LIBYA

EGYPT

Miles
0   500

Km.
0   500

Pre-war Frontiers

palacios

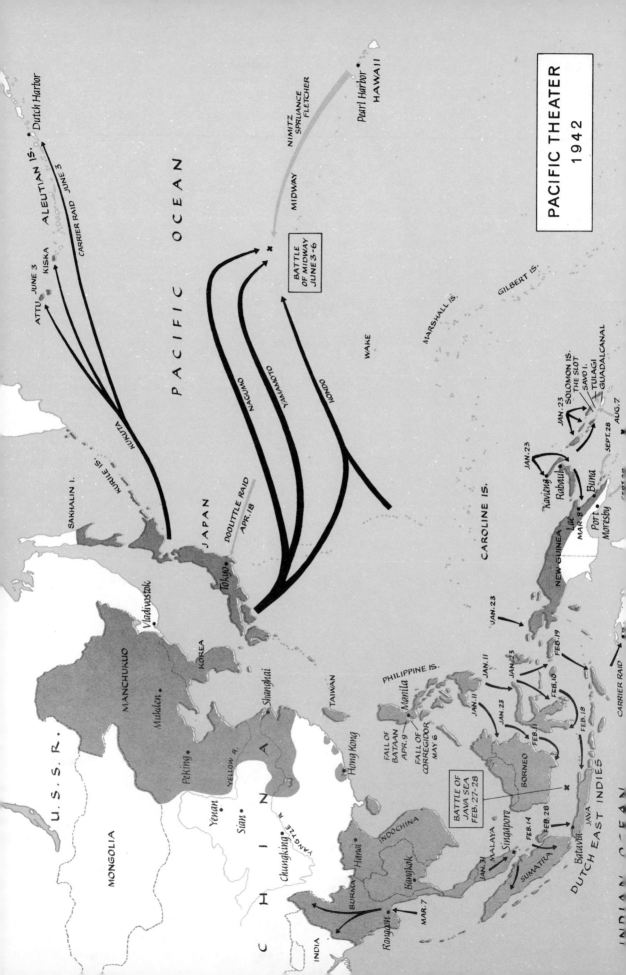

PACIFIC THEATER
1942

PACIFIC OCEAN

Dutch Harbor
ALEUTIAN IS.
KISKA JUNE 3
CARRIER RAID JUNE 3
ATTU JUNE 3
KURILE IS.
SAKHALIN I.
KURITA

NIMITZ
SPRUANCE
FLETCHER
MIDWAY
Pearl Harbor
HAWAII

BATTLE
OF MIDWAY
JUNE 3-6

WAKE

MARSHALL IS.

GILBERT IS.

NAGUMO
YAMAMOTO
KONDO

DOOLITTLE RAID
APR. 18

JAPAN

Tokyo

U.S.S.R.

Vladivostok

KOREA

MANCHUKUO

Mukden

Peking
YELLOW R.
Shanghai

MONGOLIA

Yenan
Sian
C H I N A
Chungking
YANGTZE R.

Hong Kong

TAIWAN

PHILIPPINE IS.
Manila
FALL OF
BATAAN
APR. 9
FALL OF
CORREGIDOR
MAY 6

JAN. 23
JAN. 11
JAN. 23
JAN. 11
JAN. 23
BORNEO
FEB. 11

CAROLINE IS.

NEW GUINEA
JAN. 23
FEB. 19
FEB. 10
FEB. 18
Lae
MAR. 8
Port
Moresby
Buna
Rabaul
Kavieng
JAN. 23
JAN. 23
SOLOMON IS.
THE SLOT
SAVO I.
TULAGI
GUADALCANAL
AUG. 7
SEPT. 28

BATTLE
OF JAVA SEA
FEB. 27-28

Singapore
FEB. 14
MALAYA
SUMATRA
FEB. 28
Batavia
JAVA
DUTCH EAST INDIES
CARRIER RAID

INDOCHINA
Hanoi
Bangkok
BURMA
Rangoon
MAR. 7
JAN. 31
INDIA

INDIAN OCEAN

Captives from Bataan begin the infamous Death March, marking the taking of Luzon, Philippine Islands, in April. A small garrison of Filipino-American troops continued to hold out on the tiny island of Corregidor until early May.

Australia, where, as Commander in Chief of the Allied Forces, he was to organize resistance against the Japanese. That it would take some time was evident following the disastrous battle of the Java Sea (February 27–28), in which a combined fleet of British, American, Dutch, and Australian ships, a total of fourteen, met a Japanese fleet and lost eleven. Not one Japanese ship was sunk. The virtually unopposed invasion of Java was a certainty—Japan then controlled the oil- rubber- and mineral-rich Southern Regions. On March 11, Douglas MacArthur, with his wife and young son, fled the Philippines, leaving Major General Wainwright in command. Surrender was inevitable.

The American and Filipino troops were pushed into the Bataan Peninsula and despite a high incidence of malaria and what the "battling bastards of Bataan" regarded as total neglect (it happened to be nearly true: Washington had decided to abandon the fight in the Philippines), they managed to check the Japanese for a time. Japanese reinforcements, plus supplies, at the end of March sealed the fate of the defenders. Wainwright moved his headquarters to the island of Corregidor, just two miles off Bataan, for a final stand. Major General Edward P. King surrendered on Bataan on April 9 (Wainwright's small force would hold out on Corregidor until May 6). The American-Filipino forces had held out long enough to upset the Japanese timetable, but those who had survived both battle and disease to surrender found themselves held in contempt by their captors. Over 60,000 Filipinos and 12,000 Americans were taken prisoner on Bataan and were forced to march to a prison camp at San Fernando, fifty-five miles away. The ordeal, known as the Bataan Death March, revealed a shocking Japanese brutality during the nine days of the march. Between 7,000 and 10,000 died.

On the final day of the Death March, April 18, 1942, the first good news was flashed from the Pacific. Lieutenant Colonel James H. Doolittle, one of the nation's most colorful pilots of the Twenties and Thirties, led sixteen B-25 Mitchell bombers off the tossing decks of the aircraft carrier *Hornet* in the first American attack on the Japanese homeland. Targets in Tokyo, Yokohama, Kobe, and Nagoya were bombed and, while the military effect was minimal, the implications were not lost on the Japanese High Command and the effect upon American morale was incalculable.

All aircraft were lost, fifteen when crews were forced to bail out or crash-land at night, and one, which, very low on fuel, landed in Russia, where the crew was interned (Russia and Japan were not at war). Doolittle was unaware of the impact of the raid in the United States and was certain he had failed.

To his surprise, he was promoted to the rank of brigadier general, awarded the Congressional Medal of Honor, and, eventually, would command the Twelfth, Fifteenth, and Eighth Air Forces, in turn, during the rest of the war.

Japanese military leaders were stunned and affronted; they had sworn that no enemy aircraft would sully the air over the Emperor's palace (Doolittle firmly stipulated that no bombs were to be dropped on the Imperial Palace, which was practically a religious shrine in the eyes of the Japanese people).

Losing face before the Emperor precipitated the Japanese General Staff and the Imperial Navy into a decision that would prove consequential. But once American bombers were seen in Japanese skies, it was agreed that something drastic must be done to deal with such arrogance. Admiral Yamamoto was permitted to proceed with another daring plan: the occupation of Midway Island in the Central Pacific and the invasion and occupation, with Army help, of certain key points in the Aleutian Islands off the southwestern tip of Alaska. This was to prove to be a major military consequence of the Doolittle Raid.

As a prelude to the Battle of Midway, in an effort to isolate Australia and New Zealand, the Japanese set off the battle of the Coral Sea, and in attempts to land at Tulagi, in the Solomon Islands, and Port Moresby, New Guinea. Although technically a sea battle (none of the opposing ships exchanged a shot), the Battle of the Coral Sea was fought by airmen.

The Americans, who had broken the Japanese code (the technique was called "Magic"), were aware of the impending activity in the Coral Sea and, later, somewhere in the Central Pacific. Awareness is not necessarily preparedness, especially if fighting on a shoestring, as the Americans were at the time. Admiral Chester W. Nimitz, commander of the Pacific Fleet, managed to assemble a force around two carriers, the *Lexington* and the *Yorktown*. This made the opposing carrier groups almost equal—the Japanese forces were formed around the large carriers *Shokaku* and *Zuikaku*, with a light carrier, the *Shoho*, for good measure.

The task of the Carrier Striking Force was to engage the Allied fleet (Australian ships, under British Rear Admiral J. C. Crace, were also to participate) in the Coral Sea to keep them away from the major thrust toward Port Moresby.

On May 3, although opposed, the Japanese landed troops on Tulagi. Several Japanese destroyers and smaller ships were sunk or damaged by *Yorktown* planes, but the results were not impressive and the invasion continued. The American commander of the Allied fleet, Rear Admiral Frank Jack Fletcher, broke off the Tulagi operation to concentrate on the Japanese forces in the Coral Sea.

A search plane from the *Yorktown* spotted "two carriers and four heavy cruisers" of Vice Admiral Takeo Takagi's striking group on the morning of May 7. By noon, under heavy attack by American carrier planes, the Japanese escort carrier *Shoho* sank burning in the Coral Sea.

Lieutenant Colonel James H. Doolittle, who led the mission to Tokyo, affixes Japanese medals (previously awarded to American naval officers by Japan) to the tailfins of a bomb for return to Japan.

U. S. Air Force

"Scratch one flattop!" exulted Lieutenant Commander R. E. Dixon, thus coining a popular phrase of the war. But the two, more potent flattops remained and the battle was far from over. The Japanese, meanwhile, had launched their planes which came upon two American ships, the destroyer *Sims,* which was sunk, and the oiler *Neosho,* which was so badly damaged that it was sunk by the Americans after taking off the survivors.

Crace's cruiser group was detached from the carriers and sent to cover Port Moresby. En route Crace's ships came under heavy Japanese attack but managed to escape hits while shooting down five Japanese torpedo planes.

The climax came the following day, when the opposing forces dispatched their planes. When the smoke cleared both sides claimed the victory—which could hardly be. In fact, another flattop had to be scratched, the American *Lexington.* The *Yorktown* had also been hit but not sunk; the Japanese *Shokaku* was damaged enough to preclude its participation in the approaching battle in the Central Pacific. The Japanese lost also over a hundred carrier aircraft (to the Americans' eighty-one); these aircraft and their pilots would not fight again either.

The Battle of the Coral Sea was practically a draw, except for two important facts: the Port Moresby invasion was canceled and the Japanese pilots and aircraft lost from both carriers would not participate in the Battle of Midway. Despite the lay-up of the *Shokaku,* Yamamoto

Prelude to Midway: the Battle of the Coral Sea, May 1942—the first sea battle in which surface ships did not exchange a shot. All the fighting was done by carrier-based aircraft. Although neither side could claim a clear-cut victory, the Japanese invasion attempt at Port Moresby was stopped. American Grumman Wildcats are parked on the smoldering deck of the Lexington *during the battle. The carrier, badly damaged, was later sunk.*

believed he could proceed with his plan for ridding the Pacific of the American fleet because it had been reported that both American carriers had been sunk in the Coral Sea. Yamamoto hoped that at Midway he could attend to the remaining two, the *Hornet* and the *Enterprise*.

The Americans continued meanwhile to monitor Japanese plans for the Midway operation, thanks to their ability to read Japanese coded messages. The contending sides were by no means equally matched, the Japanese enjoying the advantage of the heavier forces (if not of surprise). The Japanese had four large carriers, *Akagi, Kaga, Soryu,* and *Hiryu,* under the command of Vice Admiral Chuichi Nagumo, who had led these same carriers in the Pearl Harbor attack (Yamamoto was in over-all command of the Midway operation, which included also the proposed invasion of the North American continent in the Aleutian Islands). The American force consisted of a group of ships built around the *Enterprise* and *Hornet* (Admiral Raymond A. Spruance in command) and the battle-scarred *Yorktown* (Rear Admiral Frank J. Fletcher). Nimitz, at Pearl Harbor, was in over-all command; Yamamoto had chosen to sail with the main battle fleet aboard the new giant battleship *Yamato,* from which he would oversee the Aleutian invasion and the Midway battle. Counting the four big carriers, Yamamoto had around 200 ships of various types (including four light carriers) under his command. Nimitz had 76.

The Battle of Midway: the Yorktown *under attack by Japanese aircraft; antiaircraft bursts fill the air and geysers of water mark the misses by Japanese bombs.*

The battle opened on June 3, 1942, with Japanese carrier plane attacks on Dutch Harbor in the Aleutians; within three days landings were initiated on Kiska and Attu. Despite "Magic," the Americans had not been able to interfere with the Aleutian landings.

But, having been forewarned, Spruance had moved his carriers (he was in tactical command of both carrier groups) north of Midway before Yamamoto's line of picket submarines (which were supposed to detect American naval activity) were deployed. Yamamoto, therefore, had no idea of the presence of Spruance's little armada, nor for that matter did Spruance know just where Yamamoto was—except for the rather pointless spots in the Aleutians.

Just before dawn on June 4, after the first carrier strikes on Midway had been launched, an American search plane spotted the Japanese ships, noting the presence of at least two big carriers. As at Coral Sea, the surface ships never met; the Battle of Midway was one of the decisive air battles of the war.

Spruance, informed of the presence of Japanese ships, sped toward their location about 250 miles northeast of Midway. Meanwhile, the planes that had struck Midway Island had returned and reported that a second attack was desirable. Aircraft with torpedoes that had been ready to take off in search of American ships were detained while the torpedoes were exchanged for bombs for Midway. When this was completed, Nagumo first heard of American ships in the area; a later report mentioned a carrier.

Nagumo's fighter planes were off on patrol, his torpedo planes were armed with bombs, and the Midway strike planes were returning and had to be recovered for refueling and arming. He changed course slightly and, luckily for him momentarily, the first wave of American dive bombers did not spot his ships. Meanwhile, the harried deckhands began removing bombs and rearming the torpedo planes with torpedoes.

And then just before 9:30 that morning the first American torpedo planes materialized; for about an hour these ponderous Douglas TBD Devastators from the *Yorktown,* the *Hornet,* the *Enterprise,* and from Midway itself came in in waves and were slaughtered. Commander Fuchida, who had led the aerial attack on Pearl Harbor, observed the American attacks and later commented that all were impressed with "the dauntless courage shown by the American fliers . . . Shipboard spectators watched spellbound . . ."

And the result of the initial action strengthened their certainty of a Japanese victory at Midway. In the first three waves of the 41 American planes attacking, 35 were destroyed by antiaircraft fire or Japanese fighters (one attacking unit had missed its fighter protection in a mixup in the clouds and came in without any fighter cover). Torpedo Squadron 8, of the *Hornet,* lost all of its 15 planes.

When the thirty-fifth plane (from the *Yorktown*'s Torpedo Squadron 3, which lost 11 of its 13 Devastators) splashed into the water without hitting one Japanese ship, Nagumo, aboard his flagship, was certain Midway would soon belong to Japan. Three minutes later his reverie was shattered by a cry, "Helldivers!"

Screaming down from 19,000 feet were two squadrons of dive bombers from the *Enterprise* (Lieutenant Commander Clarence Mc-Clusky in command). The first three bombs that struck hit the deck of the *Akagi* before the stunned eyes of Nagumo.

The American Dauntlesses had appeared so suddenly that the Zero fighters that had dealt with the first wave of torpedo bombers could not rise to intercept them; antiaircraft crews were surprised—and worse, the carrier decks were crowded with aircraft being refueled or having the ordnance changed (for the third time that morning).

The flight deck of the *Akagi* became an explosive inferno, as a bomb holed the deck, which eliminated the ship as a carrier. Nagumo, under protest, was forced to leave his flagship to continue the battle from a destroyer.

Another carrier, the *Kaga,* was hit in the same attack. It too was unsalvageable and was scuttled the next day.

Yorktown dive bombers had arrived around the same time and attended to the *Soryu*. Lieutenant Commander Maxwell F. Leslie's Dive Bombing Squadron 3 placed three bombs on the deck crowded with planes being readied for takeoff, and in a moment the *Soryu* became a sheet of flame from stem to stern. Abandoned, the *Soryu* sank in the evening, its captain, Ryusaku Yanagimoto, choosing to go down with his ship.

The heavy cruiser Mikuma, *a shambles following attacks by American carrier planes, lies dead in the water. In the confusion of battle, the* Mikuma *collided with another cruiser,* Mogami, *which made them more vulnerable to air attacks. The* Mogami *struggled to the safety of Truk, but the* Mikuma *was finished off on June 6.*

Dauntless attacks leave Japanese ships burning off Guadalcanal.

The remaining Japanese carrier, the *Hiryu,* had been some distance away from the three other carriers and had escaped attack, managing to launch several dive bombers that found the *Yorktown,* scoring three hits, despite the hard-fought American interception. But some of the orphans from the *Yorktown* joined with dive bombers from the *Enterprise* and, late in the afternoon, found the *Hiryu.* Four bombs struck the wildly maneuvering carrier, blowing out the ship's island and an elevator. With the aid of Japanese torpedoes, the *Hiryu* sank the next morning.

Admiral Yamamoto was forced to digest an unequaled amount of bad news, which by dusk of that June 4 added up to a disaster for the Japanese Navy. Plans were considered to save something from the situation. Strange, optimistic messages were radioed: that the enemy fleet was practically destroyed and to prepare for the landings on Midway.

Later in the evening Yamamoto, the realist, canceled the Midway operation and prepared himself for the onerous task of apologizing to the Emperor for the defeat. He took full responsibility for the loss of 3,500 men, four fleet carriers, a heavy cruiser, and more than 300 aircraft. American losses numbered 307 men, the *Yorktown,* the destroyer *Hammann,* and 150 planes.

The Battle of Midway was the turning point of the war in the Pacific; the bubble that had been the Greater East Asia Co-Prosperity Sphere, pricked by the Doolittle Raid, was severely lanced at Midway. It has been called "The Battle That Doomed Japan"; tragically, this was not recognized; the fighting would continue for several killing years.

From their great base at Rabaul, in New Britain just northeast of New Guinea, the Japanese sent ground troops to New Guinea's northern coast, first to Lae, then Buna and Milne Bay, at the eastern tip of the island. This was a threat to Australia, a fact driven home when Japanese troops took Kokoda, halfway across the island through the Owen Stanley Range, with Port Moresby as the obvious objective. Australian troops stopped the Japanese advance in September, within 30 miles of Port Moresby. They also drove them out of Milne Bay.

In mid-September, General MacArthur sent Australian and American troops to push the Japanese back over the Owen Stanleys. As a battleground, New Guinea was undoubtedly one of the world's cruelest: tangled malarial jungles, swamps, glutinous mud, heat (and cold in the mountains), insects, and a multitude of diseases.

One of the bonuses of Midway was the first American land offensive of the war—the amphibious assault on Tulagi and Guadalcanal, in the Solomon Islands, on August 7, 1942. The tough 1st Marine Division, plus a regiment from the 2nd, established beachheads on both islands.

Guadalcanal proved easy to take, since most of the Japanese there were construction personnel working on an airfield. The field was taken by August 8 and named for Major Lofton R. Henderson, a Marine dive-bomber leader who had died in the Battle of Midway.

Coming as it had, so close to Midway, the Solomons invasion and particularly the occupation of Guadalcanal incited a strong Japanese response. The official attitude in Tokyo was that the holding of Guadalcanal was "the fork in the road which leads to victory for them or for us." This prompted the pouring in of Japanese forces, as if, indeed, the outcome of the war depended on holding one little island.

Marines came ashore at Guadalcanal unopposed by the Japanese and managed to move inland to the island's airfield before meeting opposition on August 8. Guadalcanal then erupted into a long, costly series of sea, land, and air battles.

Down the "Slot" (the waters between the several islands making up the Solomons chain) from Rabaul came the "Tokyo Express" with reinforcements and supplies, igniting a series of sea battles and prolonging the agony ashore. Initially underestimating the number of Marines (19,000 instead of 2,000 the Japanese imagined were there), Japanese troops were often wiped out on arrival.

The first delivery down the Slot was made on the morning of August 8. Because of the heavy air fighting during the day, the three American carriers that had assisted in covering the landings were withdrawn, leaving the Marines ashore with only their naval support. Unexpectedly and surprisingly, some seven Japanese ships appeared in the Slot just off tiny Savo Island. In the ensuing battle, Japanese superiority in night-fighting techniques sent four American heavy cruisers to the bottom and damaged others. It was one of the worst defeats suffered by the U. S. Navy during the war. The Japanese escaped without serious damage.

Vice Admiral Gunichi Mikawa's victory led to the practical abandonment of the Marines ashore when their naval support was also withdrawn. Supplies for only about two weeks were dumped on the shore as the ships sought safety from Japanese aerial and naval attacks. Subsisting on two meals a day, the Marines held out while Henderson Field was under final construction. The first Marine aircraft began arriving on August 20.

Japanese deliveries continued through the Slot and resulted frequently in the wiping out of the Japanese forces by the Marines. On August 24 an invasion fleet left Rabaul; it carried only 2,000 Japanese troops, but its makeup—no less than three carriers, eight battleships, six cruisers, twenty-one destroyers, and four troop transports—was intended to draw the Allied naval forces out for a decisive battle, a minor Midway.

Warned by Australian "coast watchers" (men who remained behind on various islands practically under the eyes of the Japanese), the Americans were ready, although not especially able, being in general short supply of everything. The battle of the Eastern Solomons began on August 24 and was met by American carrier planes—and the 36 Marine fighters from Henderson Field. At a loss of about 20 planes the Navy and Marine fighters accounted for nearly 90 Japanese aircraft, which decided the issue. The light carrier *Ryujo* was sunk, as were three other Japanese ships. In the fighting the *Enterprise* was damaged, which would eventually leave only the *Hornet* active in the Pacific.

The battle of the Eastern Solomons ended the daytime runs through the Slot, and the nighttime Tokyo Express was begun: fast destroyers, their decks packed with troops, would speed through the Slot under cover of darkness, deliver troops and supplies, then turn and race back to Rabaul.

As the Japanese poured in more troops, the battles raged on, around

126

and over Guadalcanal. Each arrival of the Tokyo Express stirred up bloody clashes on the island; one lasted for three days in September; the Marines fittingly named it the Battle of Bloody Ridge. In the middle of the same month the *Wasp* was sunk; at the end of October the *Hornet* (FDR's "Shangri La") was lost in the sea-air Battle of Santa Cruz, in which both sides lost heavily. By mid-October life on Guadalcanal was pure hell; Japanese battleships even shelled Henderson Field from offshore, setting fire to fuel stores, holing the muddy runways, and destroying about half the fighter strength (48 planes out of 90). But the tide had begun to turn as supplies and reinforcements, even replacements, were brought in—more Marines, a regiment of the Americal (Army) Division, and more than 200 planes.

It was not until January 7, 1943, that military wisdom prevailed and the Tokyo Express operated in reverse, slipping in during the night to take off 13,000 troops. At least 23,000 remained behind, killed or wounded in the savage fighting; American casualties were 1,592 dead, mostly Marines, and about 2,000 U. S. Navy men killed in the fighting. (Japanese naval dead are not known.) A loss of at least 600 Japanese aircraft and crews was also a serious consequence of the fruitless attempt to hold Guadalcanal, a pestilent island of little if any strategic value. Fighting in the Pacific continued in New Guinea, which by the new year would have somewhat the same outcome as that on Guadalcanal. The Japanese advance in the Pacific had been stopped.

But Japanese troops continued to hold Attu and Kiska in the Aleutians, which was chilling to Americans along the Pacific coast. This placed the enemy within reach, it was thought, of the American continent itself. Americans regarded the Japanese fighting man with fear and were at times certain that the United States would suffer an invasion. The Pacific coast rang with alarums and excursions, air-raid warnings wailed and fighter planes were dispatched to intercept "Japanese bombers" that never seemed to arrive.

And on September 9, as the fighting continued in Guadalcanal and New Guinea, a tiny Japanese plane launched from a submarine flew in the vicinity of Brookings, Oregon, and dropped incendiary bombs in a forest, with no military results. But its effect on the average American was disturbing.

Fear took many irrational forms, from merely ludicrous to the unspeakably cruel. As soon as war came "enemy aliens" of German and Italian birth were rounded up by the Justice Department, but the anti-German hysteria that had marked World War I did not ensue. Some members of the German-American Bund were jailed; in all about 3,000 Germans and less than a hundred Italians were "detained."

Japanese victories in the Pacific and scare stories of great fifth columns (boring from within) aroused anxieties and political pressures. On

Concentration camp, U.S.A. A "relocation center" for Japanese-Americans interned during the hysterical early phase of the war. This camp, located in the California mountains, was supposed to isolate the Japanese from the strategic coastal areas. Crowded, unpleasant, and demeaning, these camps were closed—protests were made by the American Civil Liberties Union and others—by the end of 1944. But the psychic scars remained.

February 19, 1942, Roosevelt had signed Executive Order 9066 to deal with the Japanese problem on the West Coast.

The voices of reason were drowned out by the harsh vocalisms of bigotry, led by the Hearst Press and the Western Growers Protective Association, a pressure group of California agriculturists who coveted the farmland owned by the Japanese-Americans.

Enforcement of Executive Order 9066 fell into the hands of Lieutenant General John L. DeWitt, head of Western Defense Command. DeWitt had already distinguished himself when he announced the presence of "30 Japanese planes over San Francisco Bay," thus inspiring some panic but even more derision. DeWitt, however, stuck to his story. He was determined to protect his command from the wily "Jap." That nothing untoward had occurred did not deter him: "The very fact that no sabotage has taken place is a disturbing and confirming indication that such action will be taken," he stated.

On March 30, DeWitt issued his own Civilian Exclusion Order No. 20, pertaining to persons of Japanese ancestry. During April and May more than 110,000 Japanese-Americans, two thirds of them legally American citizens, were rounded up and shipped to detention camps (once Roosevelt inadvertently used the term "concentration camp").

In January of 1943 word came down that the Army would accept Nisei (American-born) volunteers; immediately over a thousand enlisted. The irony was that when Nisei troops wrote home from Italy their letters were delivered to American's own concentration camps. In December 1944 this primarily racist tragedy ended when the U. S. Supreme Court decided that the western coast of the United States was no longer a "war zone," and the internees were permitted to return to their homes, provided they had any to go to.

The greater military threat, however, lay off the other coast, on the Atlantic, where German submarines hunted down Allied ships carrying supplies to Britain and eventually to Russia. The American Atlantic coast, during the early months of 1942 became a vast killing ground; a mere handful of U-boats sank dozens of ships, often within sight of spectators on shore. With Britain's warships tied up in its waters, it fell to the Americans to attempt to deal with the U-boat menace. In truth, no effective method of convoying merchant ships or protecting them from the air had been devised—which accounted for the initial string of victories for the German submarines. In painful time, the U. S. Navy developed an effective convoy system (no German U-boat was destroyed in American waters until April 1942) employing warships, aircraft, and various electronic devices. And, while the vaunted American production managed to keep ahead of the losses in the war in the Atlantic, fuel, supplies of all types were not as easily replaced. And lives not at all.

Also employed by the Germans in the Atlantic was the long-range airliner-turned-bomber, the Focke-Wulf 200 (Kondor), operating out of Norway and France; surface ships, too, were effective in the first months of the war. This phase was curtailed in May of 1941 when British warships and torpedo planes dispatched the formidable *Bismarck*. Mines were also sown in the water approaches to Britain, and these too took their toll.

But it was the U-boat that brought the Battle of the Atlantic to a crisis for the Allies. During the last half of 1942 and into the spring of 1943 the loss rate, particularly in the Atlantic, was high. (On March 11, 1943, a wolf pack sank 13 ships in one convoy; on March 20 two convoys in rather close formation lost 21 ships at the cost of one submarine.)

But that was the climax and, although U-boats would continue to operate during the rest of the war, the British-American means of dealing with the menace improved with the employment of better protected convoys and more escorts, with the use of long-range bombers, especially the Consolidated B-24 (Liberator), and radar.

Undoubtedly the most hazardous convoy route was the arctic run to Russia's northern ports, Archangel and Murmansk. In the winter Archangel was frozen in and Murmansk was the only ice-free port.

The freezing seas, high winds, and general foul weather were also formidable enemies. Men, even if dressed against the elements, came off watches so cold that the warmth of a cabin caused tearful pain.

June 1942 brought the worst disaster in the arctic run. On June 27, Convoy PQ 17, carrying aircraft, tanks, other vehicles, and cargo left Iceland. Thirty-seven cargo ships (22 of them American), with assorted escort, made way without incident until July 1, when a German plane spotted PQ 17 in the Barents Sea. U-boat attacks, because of weather, did not come until July 3, but with no harm done. However, because of a regulation of the British Admiralty, the merchant ships were soon on their own—the warships of the convoy were ordered to leave the convoy, which then faced a run of 800 miles without sufficient protection.

When the support vessels were ordered to withdraw at "High Speed" and the ships of the convoy to "disperse and withdraw to Russian ports," the way was open for the Germans to deal with PQ 17.

The National Archives

While their families were interned in "relocation centers," American-born Japanese (Nisei) volunteered for military service after January 1943, when the Army began accepting Americans of Japanese extraction. Over 30,000 served with great distinction, earning a high proportion of Purple Hearts for battle wounds. In Italy, General Mark Clark inspects Nisei troops.

Besides the convoy system, aircraft were employed to deal with German surface marauders and submarines—within the flying range of bombers. An RAF Flying Fortress flies over a convoy. A flying boat, a Short Sunderland, drops down for an attack.

Three-view of the Focke-Wulf FW-200 from a War Department Recognition Manual. The FW-200 was a transport converted into a bomber and was used in the North Atlantic as a long-range reconnaissance plane as well as for minelaying and bombing convoys.

FOCKE-WULF "F.W. 200"

SPAN: 108 ft.
LENGTH: 78 ft.

SERVICE CEILING:
30,000 ft. (not loaded)
21,500 ft. (fully loaded)

MAX. SPEED: 235 m. p. h. at 13,000 ft. (loaded)
250 m. p. h. at 13,000 ft. (bombs unloaded)

RESTRICTED

To keep the German occupation forces off balance, the British devised a special Commando force, small units that made hit-and-run raids on Occupied Europe, resulting in the destruction of German supplies, the taking of prisoners, and tying up of German troops. Most early raids were successful, such as those at St. Nazaire, in France, and at Vaagsö, Norway (December 1941); in the photo an oil installation has been set aflame. A later raid at Dieppe was a disaster, however.

The result was that the Luftwaffe, which had been quite ineffectual while the ships were in convoy, pounced. Of the 37 ships that had left Iceland as PQ 17, 11 merchant ships and two rescue ships came through. The 24 ships lost took about two thirds of the shipment to the bottom: of the 297 aircraft carried, 210 were lost; of 594 tanks, 430 were lost.

The wisdom of delaying the kind of second front that Stalin demanded was demonstrated about a month after the PQ 17 disaster. The fighting in the west was confined primarily to nighttime air raids. However, small actions were carried out against German-held France by specially trained British Commandos. Daring raids resulted in procuring German radar equipment at Bruneval, France. In March the Commandos paid an unexpected visit to the port of St. Nazaire and damaged the docks and ship berths, with satisfying success.

The cries for a second front were echoed in Britain and the United States, in response to which Combined Operations (the more proper name for the Commandos, since their operations co-ordinated land, sea,

Chief of the RAF Bomber Command (at desk) Air Chief Marshal Arthur Harris, who was certain that Germany could be knocked out of the war by aerial bombardment. With him are Air Vice Marshals R. Graham and Robert Saundby.

and air forces) proposed to attempt a rather large-scale assault on a major port which lay in Hitler's Atlantic Wall. The port selected was Dieppe.

Virtually a head-on attack was made on Dieppe early in the morning of August 19, 1942. Besides the Royal Navy ships and aircraft of the Royal Air Force, this experiment in testing the feasibility of opening the Second Front numbered also 5,000 men of the 2nd Canadian Division, a thousand British troops, and 50 American Rangers (the U.S. equivalent to the Commandos). Because the raid was to be a surprise, no heavy naval bombardment, nor air bombardment, preceded the assault.

"Operation Jubilee" did not go well. A small German convoy had spotted one group of Commandos even before the landings. Some Commandos, to the west of Dieppe, succeeded in taking out gun emplacements. But the main group at Dieppe was cut to ribbons. Less than half those who had made it ashore returned when the recall order was issued later in the day. More than two thirds of the Canadians participating in the raid were lost, killed, wounded, or captured—there were losses among the Commandos (more than 200), as well as Royal Air Force (more than a hundred planes) and the Royal Navy.

Dieppe was a debacle and, at murderous cost, it proved that a cross-Channel assault could not be attempted without true combined operations, with aerial and naval backing and sufficient equipment and planning as well.

In Russia the German campaign was quiet till June 1942. The Russian counteroffensive that saved Moscow the year before had pretty

133

much run out by February; two attempts to break the German circle around Leningrad, one in January, the other in May, failed. So did a Russian offensive in the Crimea to relieve Sevastopol; by July the city was in German hands. In the south, a Russian assault toward Kharkov in the Ukraine used up two Russian armies and hundreds of tanks. Despite their losses during the first winter of Barbarossa the Germans continued to be a tough enemy.

German reinforcements and replacements had been trained and re-equipped during the winter months and made ready for the summer offensive. The plan was to attack in the south toward Stalingrad and the oil deposits in the Caucasus. Army Group South, under the command of Field Marshal Fedor von Bock, opened the campaign on June 28. The German armies in the center and north merely remained on the defensive while the battle stormed in the south.

Outnumbered and outgunned, the Russians fell back in confusion, their leadership crumbling more as each day came and went. One German veteran was delighted: ". . . quite different from last year," he noted. "It's more like Poland."

By the second week in July the Russian High Command had formed a Stalingrad Front (an army group), sending reserves that had been concentrated near Moscow to Stalingrad on the Volga. Ordered to Stalingrad from Tula (a distance of 700 miles), General Vasili Chuikov arrived to find the city's defenders demoralized and in a daze. The news of the retreating Russian armies in the south was bad for morale.

It was about this time that Hitler told his Chief of Staff, Halder, "The Russian is finished." The usually skeptical Halder could only agree. A month later units of Army Group B had arrived at the outer defenses of Stalingrad, established on a five-mile front along the Volga just north of the city. That night of August 23, the Luftwaffe began bombing Stalingrad.

American air leaders, General Ira Eaker (left background), who commanded the Eighth Air Force in its early missions, and General Carl Spaatz, who eventually commanded all American air forces in Europe. As head of the Eighth Bomber Command, Eaker was Harris's counterpart. Eaker and Harris disagreed on the daylight vs. nighttime theory of bombardment. With Spaatz's backing Eaker prevailed and American bombers flew day missions and the British continued to bomb at night.

U. S. Air Force

Stalingrad burns after bombardment by the Luftwaffe.

In the morning the city was a ruin; virtually all of the wooden build-ings (Stalingrad was built primarily of wood) had burned. Factories were destroyed; the asphalt of paved roadways caught fire and even the Volga had been ignited when oil storage tanks detonated and their burn-ing contents flowed into the river. The water system was destroyed, in-terfering with fire fighting, and then ending it altogether. Phone com-munications went out too as telephone lines strung from burning poles fell to the burning ground. Thousands of civilians perished inside the city—but few Russian troops, for most were deployed beyond and around Stalingrad. The Luftwaffe had converted what had once been a Russian city into a Russian fortress.

For reasons difficult to rationalize Stalingrad became a German obses-sion beyond its strategic worth. Despite the Luftwaffe bombings, the city did not fall by August 25, the date Hitler had set for its occupation. He ordered General Friedrich von Paulus, commander of Army Group B's Sixth Army, to take Stalingrad. Paulus, who was the perfect Prussian with ambitions, did as he was told—only it took until September 16 be-fore his forces penetrated into the suburbs of battered Stalingrad. Rus-

135

sian resistance appeared unseemly and stubborn. This did not please Hitler, and he was even more displeased with the attitudes of some of his advisers, who warned against a new massing of Russian forces in the Stalingrad area. For voicing this truth, the outspoken Halder was called home.

Various armies (or "fronts" in Russian terminology) were forming indeed. The Stalingrad Front was under the command of General Andrey Yeremenko. In over-all command of the three fronts near Stalingrad was Marshal Georgi Zhukov, who had distinguished himself in the defense of still-beleaguered Leningrad and in the previous year's defense of Moscow and the counteroffensive.

Paulus, encouraged by promises of "a most senior post" from Hitler, continued to chip away at the ruins of Stalingrad until October 4, when he launched a head-on attack on an industrial complex in the northern part of the city: a tractor factory, an ordnance plant, and a steelworks. For nearly three weeks the fighting in the rubbled streets drained away the strength of the German army in Southern Russia.

Though outnumbered, the Russian troops could maneuver with greater effectiveness in the ruins of the city (they even got behind the Germans by moving through the sewer system). The great battle for Stalingrad had degenerated into a street-by-street, even room-by-room slaughter-fest.

By the end of October, Paulus had gained the Krasny Oktyabr (Red October) steelworks; his troops held half of the Barrikady ordnance plant and the Russians the other half; the ownership of the tractor factory was not definite. The German Sixth Army was near exhaustion to no strategic advantage, and only a trickle of reinforcements had arrived to replace the great numbers of men lost on factory floors.

Stunned troops near Stalingrad heard Hitler speak from a comfortable beer cellar on November 9. "I wanted to get to the Volga and to do so at a particular point where stands a certain town," he told members of the Nazi Party's officialdom. "By chance it bears the name of Stalin himself. I wanted to take the place, and do you know, we've pulled it off, we've got it really, except for a few enemy positions holding out . . ."

It was true, Chuikov's army was split, but fighting from isolated pockets. It was not true, however, that the Germans had Stalingrad; it had *them* and devoured them daily. This continued into November, and then on November 19, Zhukov struck. The frozen ground was right for tanks.

From the north General Konstantin Rokossovsky's troops broke through the Rumanian positions protecting Paulus's flank, swung slightly westward and continued to the south. Just south of Stalingrad, Yeremenko cut through another Rumanian army and raced to the west. Within three days Rokossovsky's and Yeremenko's troops met at

Kalach on the Don River, about forty miles *west* of Stalingrad. Paulus and his Sixth Army were enclosed in a pocket between the Volga and the Don.

Upon hearing of the unexpected development, Hitler was disquieted by the suggestion of his new Chief of Staff, Colonel General Kurt Zeitzler, that the Sixth Army be ordered to fight its way out of the encirclement before the Russians could reinforce their pincers. Hitler crashed his fist on the table and shouted, *"Ich Bleibe an der Wolga!"* (I will remain on the Volga!). What had once been a Russian fortress had become a German fortress.

Hitler was reinforced in his decision by Goering, who promised that the Luftwaffe could supply the Sixth Army by air (the minimum for the army of some 300,000 would be 500 tons of supplies a day). Having made the promise, Goering assumed it would be done—and so did Hitler; neither counted on a number of factors, including weather. Needless to say, the aerial supply route to Stalingrad was not successful; on its best day only 300 tons were delivered. Airmen and aircraft, too, were consumed by Stalingrad.

A new army, Army Group Don, was formed by Hitler, under General Erich von Manstein, to break through to Paulus and save the Sixth Army. Manstein's plan, however, called for Paulus to fight toward him as he moved toward Stalingrad; Hitler reluctantly agreed—but only if Paulus continued to hold his existing fronts. This was hardly possible. So the attempt to save the Sixth Army failed, although Manstein's troops came within 25 miles of Stalingrad. Meanwhile the Russian troops squeezed the pocket, and winter came.

The National Archives

Stalingrad, practically a total ruin, by early 1943 again belonged to the Russians. Russian troops walk through its rubble-lined streets.

Montgomery strikes back. After careful planning and waiting (to Churchill's frustration) the new desert commander lashed out late in October at El Alamein and began driving the Axis forces out of Egypt. British foot soldiers capture a Panzer III.

By January 1943 the outcome was obvious and the Russians offered Paulus the opportunity to surrender—which Hitler, who chose to remain on the Volga from a safe distance, refused. On January 24, Paulus requested permission to surrender, explaining the impossibility of further defense, without ammunition, proper clothing, fuel, and with the thousands of wounded untended. Hitler's reply was "surrender is forbidden." The Sixth Army would fight to "the last man and the last round . . ." He, in turn, explained that such a stand would contribute to "the salvation of the Western world."

Paulus was more concerned with his own personal salvation, but the pointless fighting continued. Hitler, sensing the end was near, on January 30, 1943, issued orders that Paulus be promoted to the rank of field marshal; never in the history of the German Army had a field marshal surrendered.

On January 31, 1943, Field Marshal Friedrich von Paulus made history. He surrendered to the Russian forces.

The battle of attrition at Stalingrad had consumed some 80,000 German lives (figures for Stalingrad rarely agree: another figure is 120,000); mounds of equipment, enough to furnish about 80 divisions, were lost. Russian figures are even more imprecise, but some idea of the proportionate losses might be derived from the fact that when the dead were removed from the rubble of Stalingrad for reburial, the German dead numbered 147,200 and the Russian dead (excluding civilians, many of whom fled across the Volga) 46,000. The Germans lost about five armies in their winter campaign and, although Stalingrad was not the decisive battle that some military historians claim, it had its indelible impact. It weakened the Wehrmacht in both numbers and self-esteem; the myth of the invincible German soldier was broken (although, as time would prove, he still had plenty of fight in him—even in Russia). And, if Hitler no longer placed much trust in his generals, his military omnipotence in turn no longer impressed them. In Germany itself students rioted in the streets of Munich, birthplace of the Nazi Party, in protest (the disturbance was very efficiently and brutally suppressed). The cracks had begun to appear in the Third Reich—and the German Army would never quite recover from Stalingrad. From Stalingrad on, the military initiative would lie with the confident, well-equipped, and vengeance-bound Soviet forces.

Stalin's clamoring for a second front had scant effect on the Allies, especially after the Dieppe failure; the Russian dictator did not recognize the British/American air campaign as a valid battlefront, and the African fighting seemed remote and inconclusive, a sideshow. The American Eighth Air Force began operations out of Britain with a modest attack on rail targets at Rouen, France, by a dozen Boeing B-17 Flying Fortresses on August 17, 1942. All planes bombed the target and all returned to their base safely, which many believed presaged a bright future for the Eight Air Force and its heavy daylight "precision" bombers.

The British, having learned a lesson from the one they had taught the Luftwaffe during the Battle of Britain and the opening of the Blitz, preferred to confine their actions to night—"area"—bombings. One of the major attacks by the RAF devastated the city of Cologne at the end of May. Nearly a thousand bombers, scraped up from anywhere to make the impressive number for news effect, dropped bombs into the city, seeding it with flame, desolating 600 acres, killing more than 460, injuring over 5,000, and leaving 45,000 people homeless.

RAF bomber chief Arthur Harris, although he could not repeat such a mission for some time, believed that it vindicated the heavy bomber as a weapon as well as Britain's nighttime technique.

While the Eighth Air Force gained experience, bombing targets in France, primarily connected with submarine operations, it was learned that not all targets were vulnerable to heavy bombardment, especially in small numbers. Sub pens were ringed with antiaircraft guns and protected by German fighters.

Although British Bomber Command had begun attacking targets inside Germany, American Flying Fortresses and Liberators concentrated on nearer objectives in France. American bombers would not attempt a flight to Germany until 1943. One of the reasons was that some of the most experienced crews had been drawn away for the North African campaign.

Like Stalin, Hitler looked upon North Africa as a second-rate venture

Torch invasion units converge on North Africa; some ships came directly from the United States and most from Britain. The mixed American-British assault force was under the command of American Lieutenant General Dwight D. Eisenhower. Smaller ships patrol for German or Italian submarines.

which, he was certain, he could leave in the capable hands of the miracle-man, Rommel. Such faith would hardly have impressed Rommel, who felt it should also be backed up with supplies and men. Mussolini, too, left the fate of his troops in German hands. Both Axis leaders, in studying their war maps, appeared only to see the northern top of Africa, apparently unaware of all that water just above and what it implied—the Mediterranean Sea. For this oversight, Mussolini would be the first to suffer. The British, a nation of seamen, recognized the importance of the sea—for it was the route to India and the Far East. The Balkans, with oil that the Wehrmacht required, were also a consideration; and in the Mediterranean were the strategically placed islands of Crete, in German control, and Malta, suffering almost daily bombing by the Axis.

As if to prove his two masters correct, Rommel succeeded in taking Tobruk, which had held out for so long, on June 21, 1942. On June 25 he swept further into Egypt to take El Alamein; the next day he was elevated by Hitler to the rank of field marshal. But, his lines were stretched too far, and his troops too tired. Rommel was held by the British, who were also exhausted. Both sides dug in around El Alamein to recover.

There was unhappiness in the British camp following the failure in

June of the "Cauldron" operation and then the stalemate at El Alamein; the inevitable shakeup followed. On August 13, Lieutenant General Bernard L. Montgomery arrived to take command of the rather tattered Eighth Army; "Monty," as he was called by his troops, was rarely troubled by self-doubts. Two days later, General Sir Harold Alexander succeeded Auchinleck as Commander in Chief, Middle East Land Forces; his task was to destroy the Rommel legend and, of course, the German-Italian forces in Africa.

Montgomery's initial job was to reorganize the Eighth Army. There was a subtle political necessity, also. Churchill's government needed a solid victory after the fall of Singapore, the loss of Burma, and the general air of failure in Africa at the moment.

Montgomery was a careful planner, a "bleak realist," and a believer in tough preparation for battle: training and the amassing of supplies. During the initial phase of Montgomery's preparations, Rommel attempted to break through the British defenses at the Alam Halfa Ridge and was forced to withdraw. Though it was no great victory for Montgomery, the British had held and he proceeded with his plans. When September came and went, Montgomery had not yet begun "to tidy up the battlefield." While all was not quiet on the desert, it was not very active, either. During the lull Rommel, ill, returned to Germany for rest and medical treatment. Montgomery, meanwhile, treated his troops to an intensive training program and accumulated tanks, guns, aircraft, supplies, and more troops. He scorned the romantic trust in luck and battlefield dash.

If war was a sporting event (as some military romantics appear to believe), then the second battle of El Alamein was not fairly executed. War is, after all, not an art but the inexact science of killing, of destroying your opponent and his tools. You accomplish this by exploiting every advantage and, as he recorded in his neatly written notes for a prebattle speech to senior officers, Montgomery's aim was to "shoot tanks and shoot Germans."

When he unleashed the offensive he called "Lightfoot," Montgomery enjoyed about a two-to-one advantage over Rommel's forces: over a thousand tanks (including a couple of hundred new American Sherman tanks, the equal of any German tank then in Africa); Rommel had less than 500 tanks (preponderantly Italian). The Axis troops had about half the guns of all types compared with the British supply. It was the same with troops—about 195,000 British to about 100,000 Axis (85 British infantry battalions against 30 German and 40 Italian). British aircraft easily dominated the battlefield.

Montgomery was even in better health than his opponent, who was in Austria when the second battle of El Alamein erupted with the roar of more than a thousand big guns in the morning of October 23, 1942, along the front. This was a line, which the Germans and the Italians had mined and dug into, that ran from the Mediterranean in the north to the Qattara Depression in the south, a front of about forty miles. The tactics of the past in the desert would not work: the end run around the southern tip of the enemy's line. The treacherous quicksands below the Qattara made that impossible—for both sides. Montgomery chose to attack in the northern section of the line. The artillery barrage would clear out most of the mines.

During the initial phase of Montgomery's attack, General Georg Stumme, deputy commander of the Axis troops in Rommel's absence, died on the battlefield—of a heart attack.

In his hospital room far from the battle Rommel was kept informed by Field Marshal Keitel, Chief of the Army High Command. The two agreed that Rommel would return to Africa "if necessary." The commander of commanders, Hitler called twice decreeing, "with regret," that it *was* necessary. "I took off next morning [October 24]," Rommel wrote. "I knew there were no laurels to be earned in Africa."

Lightfoot was not proceeding as planned, and it appeared as if Montgomery would gather few laurels himself, for the attack had bogged down in the battle zone. Unperturbed, Montgomery revised his plans, which led to some battlefield confusion, but he continued to push. Rommel's attempts to counterattack were stopped by antitank fire and air attack. Even so, Montgomery's initial plan had failed; the Alamein line held.

On November 1, Montgomery threw in a reserve he had nurtured; although losses were high on both sides, numbers decided the issue. Drawing upon his vast resources, Montgomery pressured Rommel (then down to about thirty tanks), who began to withdraw. Rommel soon received the typical Adolf Hitler order: ". . . victory or death . . ." for his troops. This order was observed for twenty-four hours, and then Rommel, no Paulus, ordered the retreat to resume. With the Panzer Army racing for safety, Montgomery was slow to pursue (such caution, many believe, kept him from a more total victory at Alamein).

Pure victory or not, Montgomery had shattered the legend of the Desert Fox and assured the security of the Suez Canal and Malta. Losses were high. The Allies lost 13,500 dead and wounded, to the Axis 26,000—mostly Italian; Montgomery lost more tanks than Rommel had at the beginning of the battle.

Rommel continued pulling back—out of Egypt, across Cyrenaica, in Libya, until by the end of the year, with supply lines stretched tightly, the Eighth Army ran out of steam. Rommel dug in at Bureat el Hsur, beyond Sirte, where the Eighth also burrowed. By this time, something had happened farther westward that Rommel felt "spelled the end of the Army in Africa."

*A combined Anglo-British force landed near Algiers,
although the American flag was prominently displayed
to encourage French aid. This did not always work and
there were clashes with the North African French.*

*Rommel, as usual, in the vanguard of battle
to exploit any advantage. In June 1942 he
began moving toward Tobruk.*

In North Africa you will meet the descendants of races and empires which were making history at the dawn of organized life, thousands of years ago. Some of the people are Arabs, some Negroes, some of other origins.

* * *

They are not backward, uneducated people. They were great, and created rich cultures long before Columbus discovered America.

* * *

These words from a pamphlet entitled *North Africa* ("For All Members of United States Expeditionary Forces in North Africa") were read by American troops about to take part in "Operation Torch," the Anglo-American answer to Stalin's second-front demands—a full-scale invasion of North Africa in French Morocco and Algeria.

The invasion was under the command of Lieutenant General Dwight D. Eisenhower to give it a predominantly American cast. The French continued to hold a grudge against the British for what they had done to the French Navy at Oran in 1940. The Americans, it was hoped, would be welcomed as liberators. But when the landings began on November 8, 1942, the Stars and Stripes, conspicuously in the vanguard, did not eliminate French resistance altogether. A naval encounter between American and French ships off Casablanca resulted in the deaths of nearly 500 French seamen. Troops wading ashore at the invasion areas centered on Casablanca, in Morocco, and at Oran and Algiers (by British troops), in Algeria, were opposed but halfheartedly, and by November 11 the Allies were firmly established in French North Africa. At about the same time Rommel's troops were racing back through fabled Tobruk, with Montgomery in relentless, if not speedy, pursuit. Rommel was in a squeeze, with Eisenhower approaching from the west and Montgomery from the south and east.

Their common objective was Tunisia, into which German reinforcements were being ferried from Italy. By December the push from the west was stopped by Rommel at Medjez-el-Bab, Tunisia. It was obvious that the Germans were not yet done in North Africa, but it was equally obvious, as Rommel himself had realized, that it was a matter of time.

Churchill's year of struggle and peril ended with the tide definitely turned against the Axis: in North Africa, in Russia, and in the Pacific.

Japanese infantry move forward on Bataan, January 1942. The Japanese soldier proved to be tough, resourceful, and a formidable jungle fighter.

A Japanese light tank smashes a pathway through the Philippine jungle on Bataan Peninsula, into which Filipino-American forces under General Douglas MacArthur were being forced by the victorious Japanese.

Japanese invasion money printed for use in British colonies and possessions.

Strange cargo: U. S. Army Air Force B-25 Mitchell bombers on the deck of the carrier Hornet, *trailed by two escort ships. The target: Tokyo. The time: April 1942, gloomy, cheerless, and all but hopeless.*

One of Doolittle's Raiders passes over the Yokosuka Naval Base on Tokyo Bay south of the capital. Photo was taken by then Lieutenant Richard A. Knobloch, co-pilot of the thirteenth plane. Knobloch was the only participant who did not lose his camera, and the only one to bring back photos of the Tokyo raid.

Before the battle: wings folded, Navy dive bombers are spotted on a carrier deck. The blackboard informed pilots taking off of pertinent data. A bomb rests on the deck.

There were American losses at Midway: the Yorktown, *hit by Japanese bombers, was finally sunk by a Japanese submarine torpedo.*

Douglas SBD Dauntlesses ready for takeoff from a carrier deck. The courage of Dauntless crews in the face of deadly antiaircraft fire and Japanese Zero fighters was phenomenal and decided the outcome of the Battle of Midway.

Still from a Navy film made during the Battle of Midway, June 1942. Dauntlesses moving in on the Japanese fleet, one ship of which burns below them.

The hazards of carrier life. Landing a plane on a moving deck was a delicate operation and not always successful, especially if the pilot was injured or the plane damaged. Such landings as this resulted, often with devastating results. The crewmen, however, walked away from this landing.

The Tokyo Express provides fodder for the Battle of Bloody Ridge, a Japanese attempt to take the Marines' Henderson Field, September 12–14. These Japanese had infiltrated the Marine lines during the night, but like their comrades were killed. More than 600 Japanese were lost in this attempt.

The Japanese response to the American landings at Guadalcanal was to pour troops into the island and to make heavy sea and air attacks. These Japanese troops, making a nighttime attack across the strongly held Marine positions on the Tenaru River on August 20. Machine-gun fire annihilated nearly an entire Japanese battalion.

The National Archives

The battle for Guadalcanal, Solomon Islands, opens on August 7, 1942, with the launching of carrier-borne air strikes and naval bombardment. A bomb-laden Dauntless leaves the deck of a carrier.

The waters around Guadalcanal boiled with sea and carrier battles as the Japanese attempted to run reinforcements in by the Tokyo Express and the Americans tried to stop them as well as reinforce and supply the embattled Marines. On convoy escort duty to the Solomons, the carrier Wasp *was hit by three torpedoes from a Japanese submarine and went down on September 15.*

A Japanese Mitsubishi Type 97, more popularly known as "Sally"—the code name assigned to it by American Intelligence. A heavy bomber, it could also be used as a transport.

Once firmly established on Guadalcanal, American troops employed Solomon Islanders in various construction jobs, repair work, and other chores. A work crew prepares for a ride to the job.

Aircraft-recognition silhouette of the clipped wing "Zeke" (or Zero), which was, for a time, code-named "Hap"—until noted by Air Force commander General Arnold, whose nickname was Hap. The plane, which was active in the Solomons, was very quickly renamed "Hamp."

"HAP" TYPE 0 MK.2 F

SPAN: 36 ft.
LENGTH: 28 ft.
APPROX. SPEED: 338 m. p. h. at 17,200 ft.

SERVICE CEILING: 38,800 ft.

RESTRICTED

Zero fighters escorted the Japanese bombers on their missions to Guadalcanal from the great Japanese bases at Rabaul, New Britain. This created a fuel problem for the fighter pilots, who had little time for fighting in the Solomons; if they lingered, not enough fuel remained for the return to Rabaul.

A rare sight: Japanese prisoners, Guadalcanal. Captivity was regarded with loathing by the Japanese, who preferred death, even by suicide, than to be taken prisoner.

A German submarine crew based at Spitsbergen, Norway, for operations against British convoys on the northern run to Russia.

A surfaced German submarine under attack by a Sunderland.

The Nazi Propaganda Ministry's view of the alliance of Britain, the United States, and Russia: "Behind the enemy powers: the Jew." The profiteering, cynical, manipulative Jew was a favorite subject of the German propaganda mill.

Hinter den Feindmächten: der Jude

The summer campaign opens in Russia, moving, in the south, toward Stalingrad. Russian troops under German artillery fire fall back.

German panzers enter Sevastopol, in the Crimea, as refugees leave. July 1942.

Red Army scouts in the Caucasus, which Hitler hoped to reach before summer's end to cut off the supply of Soviet oil. He came close and then became obsessed with Stalingrad.

Trench dug by Stalingraders for the defense of their city; results of German bombardment can be seen in background ruins.

Nazi flag marks a German position in Stalin-grad; Russian troops probably occupy the riddled building opposite.

Field Marshal Friedrich von Paulus, who led the victorious Sixth Army to Stalingrad and then found himself surrounded by the Russians. Ordered to hold his position by Hitler, Paulus was in a hopeless state with the coming of winter. To Hitler's displeasure, he became the first German field marshal in history to sur-render.

The major American heavy bomber of 1942, the Boeing Flying Fortress.

Primary weapon of the British strategic bombardment offensive, the Avro Lancaster heavy bomber. It was one of the most effective bombers of the war.

Rommel beams at his smiling superior, Italian Marshal Attore Basico.

Italian tanks on the move.

Afrika Korpsman signals to his gun crew in the Western Desert. Rommel was on the move again.

An 88 gun crew zeroes in on British tanks and troops.

A Free French patrol in the desert around Bir Hacheim, which lay in the path of Rommel's summer thrust toward Tobruk and El Alamein.

Free French troops. Though they fought gallantly at Bir Hacheim, they had to withdraw under Rommel's pressure.

Removing a land mine, gingerly. Both sides used mines that were buried under the sand in great fields, making moving through open spots in the desert extremely dangerous. Serious injuries resulted from stepping on mines—and they could blow a track off a tank.

The summer war in the desert was grim for the British, who lost heavily under Rommel's attacks—the Bir Hacheim-El Gazala line gave way, Tobruk fell, and Rommel pushed on by July to El Alamein. British prisoners of war are being driven behind the lines for detention.

Photo by Rommel: a fallen British soldier.

Montgomery's infantry takes a German gun position.

Afrika Korps cemetery, North Africa, 1942.

Major General George Patton boards a landing craft for the race to the beaches of North Africa.

D-Day, North Africa, November 8, 1942. Depth charges discourage the incursion of enemy submarines.

Landing operations, North Africa; an LCM—Landing Craft, Mechanized— is being readied to be put over the side for loading and the run for landing areas.

An American 105-howitzer crew dashes inland from the beach, North Africa.

With Anglo-American troops firmly lodged in North Africa and moving east-ward, these Douglas A-20 Havocs fly over the Tunisian desert seeking Axis targets.

A Landing Ship, Tank (LST) disgorges a Sherman tank, one of the out-standing vehicles of the war. Mass-produced, it was used by the Americans and British.

General Patton on land near Casablanca, overseeing the landing operations. A colorful figure, he sports his famed brace of pearl-handled pistols.

Montgomery's troops, moving in on Rommel from the east, squeezed the Afrika Korps into Tunisia. RAF bombers cut off Rommel's supply lines by bombing African ports. A German ammunition ship has been bombed in the harbor at Benghazi, Libya. By November 20, Montgomery's Eighth Army took Benghazi; for the Afrika Korps it was the beginning of the end.

1943

Deeds of Carnage

T HE YEAR BEGAN with promise for the Allies, except in the U-boat-infested Atlantic. The Australians and Americans had retaken Buna in New Guinea; the Germans were withdrawing from the Caucasus, if not Stalingrad; the Tokyo Express was running in reverse at Guadalcanal, and the Allies were firmly established in North Africa.

Eisenhower was then confronted not only with a military situation with untried American troops, but also with sensitive diplomatic-personality perplexities with the French. The sunny-dispositioned (at least in public) Eisenhower proved himself as a diplomat-soldier early in North Africa. He encouraged a healthy spirit of co-operation with the British and adroitly handled the French situation. Because Admiral of the Fleet Jean Darlan, a Vichyite who had co-operated with the Germans, encouraged the French in North Africa to cease fighting and join with the Allies, it was decided that he should be placed in charge of French affairs in North Africa.

Eisenhower's decision was severly criticized in Britain and in the United States—the thought of dealing with a supporter of Hitler's plan for a "New Europe" on equal terms was anathema. Nor did it please the man who visualized himself as the savior of France, Charles de Gaulle (who had been sentenced to death *in absentia* by the collaborators of Vichy).

By Christmas of 1942 the Darlan aspect of the problem was solved when a young Frenchman assassinated Darlan. He was replaced by General Henri Giraud, commander of the French forces in North Africa. Taken prisoner by the Germans in 1940, Giraud had escaped, made his way to Vichy, and eventually to North Africa. Giraud, although not tainted by Vichy, was not regarded with equanimity by de Gaulle.

Deep frost in North Africa: General Henri Giraud, President Roosevelt, General Charles de Gaulle, and Prime Minister Churchill in a posed photograph to demonstrate Allied unity. De Gaulle could not accept Giraud as supreme commander of the French forces (a role he coveted himself).

Nor did de Gaulle look upon Churchill and Roosevelt with enchantment, for they had managed the whole Torch operation without him (both had anticipated de Gaulle's demands and preferred to keep him in the dark until after the event).

By early January the North African front was sufficiently secure so that a dramatic meeting was arranged for Churchill, Roosevelt, and their staffs (Stalin declined, saying he was too busy with the war) at Casablanca, Morocco. A number of critical decisions were made which would affect the conduct of the war; behind-the-scenes friction was dissembled by a photograph of de Gaulle and Giraud tentatively clasping hands. After ten days the Allied chiefs had agreed to step up the war on the submarines (which threatened supplies for the battlefronts), to push the Germans out of Africa, and then to move into Sicily and Italy itself (the American military leaders did not agree with the British on this move but were argued down). Planning was to begin on the return to Europe across the English Channel (Stalin was then informed that there would be no second front in Europe in 1943).

At Casablanca, Major General Ira C. Eaker, commander of the U. S. Eighth Air Force met with Churchill and convinced him that American

168

EUROPE
1943

ARCTIC OCEAN

BARENTS
SEA

N

Petsamo

Murmansk

Archangel

ATLANTIC
OCEAN

U.S.S.R.

SWEDEN

FINLAND

VOLGA R.

NORWAY

Leningrad

Oslo

Helsinki

Moscow

Stockholm

EST.

NORTH SEA

LATVIA

Bryansk

DON R.

PAULUS
SURRENDERS
JAN. 31/43

DENMARK

BALTIC
SEA

LITH.

Kursk

Belgorod

Stalingrad

IRELAND

Warsaw

Wilhelmshaven

Hamburg

VISTULA R.

POLAND

Kiev

Poltava

DONETS R.

ENGLAND

Emden

ELBE R.

Rostov

London

Schweinfurt

Berlin

DNEPER R.

CAUCASUS

RUHR

GERMANY

CRIMEA

Kassel

RHINE R.

Paris

Regensburg

CZECHOSLOVAKIA

BLACK SEA

FRANCE

SEINE R.

Vienna

ROMANIA

LOIRE R.

HUNGARY

Ploesti

AUSTRIA

Bucharest

Vichy

SWITZ.

Ankara

RHONE R.

ITALY

ADRIATIC
SEA

YUGOSLAVIA

BULGARIA

DANUBE R.

TURKEY

MUSOLINI
RESCUED
SEPT. 12

Termoli

Foggia

ALBANIA

CORSICA

Rome

Bari

Taranto

GREECE

Naples

Salerno

Athens

Madrid

SPAIN

SARDINIA

SICILY

CRETE

Gibraltar

Bizerte

Tunis

MALTA

PANTELLERIA

MEDITERRANEAN SEA

Alexandria

VON ARNIM
SURRENDERS

Enfidaville

Faid

KASSERINE PASS

Gafsa

Medenine

EGYPT

Casablanca

MARETH
LINE

Tripoli

MONTGOMERY

MOROCCO

ALGERIA

LIBYA

| 0 | Miles | 500 |
| 0 | Km. | 500 |

Pre-war Frontiers

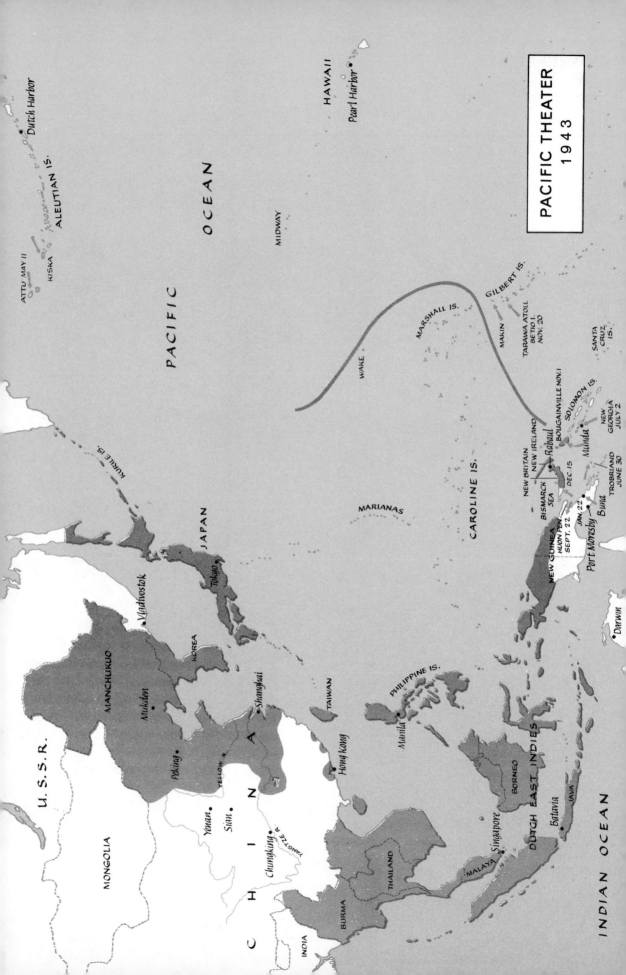

PACIFIC THEATER
1943

PACIFIC OCEAN

HAWAII
Pearl Harbor

Dutch Harbor
ALEUTIAN IS.
ATTU MAY 11
KISKA

MIDWAY

WAKE

MARSHALL IS.

GILBERT IS.
MAKIN
TARAWA ATOLL
BETIO I.
NOV. 20

SANTA
CRUZ
IS.

CAROLINE IS.

MARIANAS

KURILE IS.

JAPAN

Tokyo

Vladivostok

KOREA

MANCHUKUO

Mukden

Peking

YELLOW R.

Shanghai

Hong Kong

TAIWAN

PHILIPPINE IS.

Manila

BORNEO

DUTCH EAST INDIES

Batavia

JAVA

SOLOMON IS.
NEW
GEORGIA
JULY 2
Munda
BOUGAINVILLE NOV. 1
New Ireland
Rabaul
NEW BRITAIN
DEC. 15
BISMARCK
SEA
JAN. 22
TROBRIAND
JUNE 30
Buna
NEW GUINEA
HUON PEN.
SEPT. 22
Port Moresby

Darwin

U.S.S.R.

MONGOLIA

Yenan
Sian
Chunking
YANGTZE R.

C H I N A

BURMA

THAILAND

MALAYA
Singapore

INDIA

INDIAN OCEAN

daylight precision bombardment should not be abandoned. He argued that American bombers by day and British by night ("bombing around the clock," a phrase Churchill picked up and used in Parliament) would disrupt German defenses and result in fewer losses by the Allies.

On the final day of the conference Roosevelt made a general statement that would have later repercussions. "The elimination of German, Japanese, and Italian war power means the unconditional surrender of Germany, Italy and Japan," he said in part. "It does not mean the destruction of the population of Germany, Italy or Japan, but it does mean the destruction of the philosophies in those countries which are based on conquest and the subjugation of other people." The term "unconditional surrender" immediately overshadowed the point of the last sentence and later Roosevelt was accused of prolonging the war because the peoples of Germany and Japan fought more desperately out of fear of the consequences of defeat, an unlikely and dubious presumption.

By the time he left Casablanca on January 16, plans had been made by Eisenhower, in conference with British Generals Sir Alan Brooke and Alexander, to make a co-ordinated attack (with Montgomery's Eighth Army) on Tunisia—at that very moment filling up with supplies and reinforcements for Rommel.

Montgomery continued his pressure from the east and, passing through Tripoli, the main Axis port in Libya, continued on into Tunisia, turning northward, and was stopped momentarily at a strongpoint at Mareth in mid-February. Although Montgomery had kept Rommel on the run, he had not succeeded in catching him. From the west, also pressing into Tunisia, the British Fourth Army and units of the U. S. II Corps had established a wide front running from the sea at Cape Serrat southward toward Montgomery's position.

On February 14 the canny Desert Fox struck, employing the supplies and troops Hitler had so begrudgingly sent him. Rommel had selected a weak spot in the line held by green American troops in the south-central part of the line at Faid. Overwhelmed by superior and more experienced forces, the American troops fell back. Rommel, hoping to create a great gap between Anglo-American forces in the north and Montgomery's Eighth Army in the south, pressed the attack. The Afrika Korps poured through Faid and Gafsa, pushing the retreating Americans back nearly fifty miles, into narrow Kasserine Pass. The German-Italian forces overran forward air bases; there were heavy American casualties and loss of supplies and equipment.

Rommel had even begun to consider the possibility of pushing the Allies back to Algeria. But Allied reinforcements, British, French, and American, were dispatched to Kasserine; also, Rommel's supply line had begun to stretch thin—and he did not have the full co-operation of his Afrika Korps commander, Colonel General Jurgen von Arnim, who

An American Sherman tank, well armed and armored, proved a formidable challenger to the Afrika Korps' Panzers in North Africa. Its maximum speed was about 23 miles an hour and mounted a 75-mm. gun and two machine guns.

American M-3 medium tank, named the Stuart by the British. About ten miles an hour faster than the heavier Sherman, the Stuart was used by Patton's men in North Africa.

disagreed with the plan for pushing the Allies back to Algiers. By February 23, Rommel's drive had run down and three days later the Allies rallied and fought the Germans back to the original line. The Rommel blitz had tested the Allies, especially its commanders under confusion and stress, and the Allies had proved themselves.

Frustrated, Rommel struck out in another direction from the Mareth Line at Médenine on March 6; this attempt to drive Montgomery back failed also. Later in the month, Montgomery dealt with the Mareth Line by swinging around it, outflanking the Axis forces, and pressing hard.

By March 24, Axis troops had begun to withdraw into Tunisia; the writing was on the wall. Its message was clearly obvious on April 7, when Montgomery's Eighth Army linked up with units of the U. S. II Corps in Tunisia.

For the final push the Allies regrouped and transferred some of Montgomery's best troops to the U. S. First Army. Lieutenant General Sir Harold Alexander, Eisenhower's deputy, was placed in command of this newly constituted Eighteenth Army Group. On May 1 a line of about 120 miles ran from Bizerte in the north and curved downward and eastward to Enfidaville; squeezed inside was what remained of the vaunted Afrika Korps and the Italian First Army. Harried by artillery fire, bombardment from the air, and lack of supplies (the Allies sank the ships and shot cargo planes out of the skies wholesale), the Axis line cracked by May 6, the next day the Americans were in Bizerte and the British in Tunis. Rommel turned his command over to Arnim and, still ailing, flew out of Tunisia to Germany.

On May 13 the last Axis survivor who could fled, but some 240,000 Axis troops (nearly half of them Germans) surrendered to the Allies. Arnim represented the Germans, and Marshal Giovanni Messe, nominally Arnim's superior, brought an end to Mussolini's dream of conquest.

Early in March, Josef Stalin issued an order of the day celebrating the twenty-fifth anniversary of the Red Army. With characteristic grace he stated in the order: "In view of the absence of a second front in Europe the Red Army alone is bearing the whole weight of the war." The Allies, as if in answer to this casuistry, began preparing for just that. Allied bombers mounted heavy attacks on Sicily, which lay between Tunisia and Italy (held by nearly 300,000 troops, mostly Italian); the Italian mainland was bombed also, as were the islands of Sardinia and Pantelleria (the latter halfway between Tunisia and Sicily, an excellent fighter base). Pantelleria was taken on June 11 practically unopposed, the first time a military objective was taken out virtually by air power alone.

"Operation Husky," Montgomery's plan for taking Sicily, was under the over-all command of Alexander. Montgomery's Eighth Army was to

May 7, 1943: American troops mopping up inside Bizerte, Tunisia.

land on the southeastern tip of the island, near Syracuse. Lieutenant General George S. Patton's Seventh Army would invade at Gela on the southwestern coast. D-Day was to be July 10; this was preceded by heavy Allied bombings to confuse the Axis. Early morning Allied airborne assaults went somewhat awry because of high winds, but the amphibious landings went virtually as planned—though Patton's troops ran into the tough Hermann Goering Division, plus two Italian divisions, near Gela, which held up their advance for a while.

The British drove northward, capturing Syracuse on July 12 as the Americans spread through western Sicily; on July 22 Patton was in Palermo, on the northern coast. The race for Messina, just opposite Italy, was on. Three days later a surprising political note was struck when the Italian Fascist Grand Council forced Mussolini to resign from office. Marshal Pietro Badoglio became Premier and King Victor Emmanuel III commander of Italy's armed forces.

The Axis troops were driven into the northeast corner of Sicily, at Messina, where evacuation was possible—although not without interference from Allied bombers. The Germans fought fiercely (most Italian troops began surrendering in droves by the end of July) but halted the Allies only temporarily. Patton drove his Seventh Army, hoping to beat Montgomery to Messina. After taking Palermo, American morale lifted and the memory of Kasserine Pass faded. On the morning of August 17, as the last of the German defenders slipped across the Strait of Messina, Patton's advance patrols entered the city. Mont-

174

gomery followed shortly after; Sicily had taken thirty-eight days to fall completely into Allied hands.

The German troops, outnumbered, had fought hard, inflicting severe casualties on the Allies; with Italy the obvious next objective, the German determination to make it a battleground did not bode well for the Allies. With Mussolini out of power the surrender of Italy was a matter of time (and complex negotiations); Hitler moved quickly. Under Rommel, German troops began moving into Northern Italy and those already there dug in. Italy would not prove to be the "soft underbelly" of Europe that Churchill claimed it would be.

There was a major strategic disagreement over the proposed invasion of Italy: the British wished to wage a full-scale war in the Mediterranean, the Americans wanted to plan for an early spring cross-Channel assault on Hitler's *Festung Europa.* Each side conceded and the Italian invasion was on, but as soon as the battle for Sicily was over, four American and three British divisions were withdrawn from the Mediterranean and sent to Britian to prepare for "Operation Overlord," the code name for the invasion of Europe. Italy became a kind of second-rate second front.

Two divisions of Montgomery's Eighth Army crossed the Strait of Messina on the night of September 3, 1943. (On this same day the Italians signed an armistice secretly so as not to arouse their German ally;

Husky on schedule; Patton's troops went ashore at Gela with little opposition initially, but suffered heavy casualties in later waves. The cruisers Boise *and* Savannah *took out the Italian-German shore batteries to clear the way.*

Invasion chiefs: Admiral Alan G. Kirk, commander of the U. S. Amphibious Force, Atlantic Fleet; Lieutenant General George Patton, commander of the U. S. Seventh Army and over-all commander of the Sicilian operation, General Sir Harold Alexander.

Eisenhower announced the fact publicly on September 8, by which time Montgomery was firmly established in Southern Italy).

A larger force, Lieutenant General Mark W. Clark's Fifth Army, was to land 180 miles north of the toe of Italy at Salerno on September 9. The Germans were waiting for them. While the battle raged, Field Marshal Albert Kesselring, commander of the German forces in Italy, ordered the occupation of Rome, supposedly an "open city," and designated Italy a war theater under German control.

Despite obstacles—blown bridges and tunnels—Montgomery moved northward and Clark's troops fought out of the beachhead at Salerno. By September 13 the two forces linked up; Naples was occupied on October 1. The British 1st Airborne Division moved into the naval base at Taranto. Bari, an important port on the Adriatic coast, also fell, as did the great complex of air bases farther north at Foggia. By mid-October the Allies had established a solid front across Italy, north of Naples on

After the successful landings at Sicily, three days of heavy enemy aerial attack ensued, which took a toll of the naval units offshore. An American ammunition ship, hit by a German bomber attack, goes up in a spectacular blast.

the west coast to Termoli on the east, just north of Foggia. On October 13, Italy declared war on Germany.

The Germans were also solidly entrenched above the Allied line in their own Gustav Line. With the coming of winter the Italian campaign became cruel and static, lashed by rains, bogged down by mud. The tourist's term "Sunny Italy" became a grim joke; so did Churchill's "soft underbelly," which proved to be instead a hard, sawtoothed spine.

Taking Foggia added a further dimension to the Mediterranean war; it would enable the Allies to establish another strategic air force, the Fifteenth, in order to intensify the air war against Germany.

The American effort from England, as the year opened, was aimed primarily against U-boat targets in France. On January 27, 1943, the Eighth Air Force managed to get up 91 Flying Fortresses and Liberators to strike a target on German soil for the first time: the submarine yards at Wilhelmshaven; of these aircraft, 53 bombed the target—two others dropped bombs on U-boats at Emden and three were lost. Poor weather deterred not only the American bombers, nearly half of which did not bomb at all, but also the Luftwaffe fighter planes. The mission was not especially successful, although the small loss was encouraging—and the fact that the Americans had begun to reach into Germany proper was good for morale.

British Bomber Command had been bombing German targets since 1940, dating roughly from the period of the Blitz. These were initially little more than raids, but under "Bomber" Harris, the attacks by night grew heavier and German industrial cities began to suffer, as did their populations.

The RAF broke momentarily with its nighttime policy with an audacious daytime attack on Berlin—a spite raid whose primary mission was to break up Hitler's tenth-anniversary celebration of his coming into power on January 30. The real aerial Battle of Berlin began about this same time—with consequent reprisal bombings of London—and did not let up until the war ended. The bombings of the Nazi capital were carried out by Bomber Command at night; the Eighth Air Force did not join in until March 1944.

Hitler's contempt and distrust for the Luftwaffe was further aggravated in July by a series of day-and-night attacks on Hamburg by the Eighth Air Force and Bomber Command. The RAF came over during

Sicily was a steppingstone into Italy, the major prize of the Allies in the Mediterranean. The British Eighth Army moved into the toe of Italy across the Strait of Messina early in September; on the ninth, the American Fifth Army began landings at Salerno, where in general the assault went smoothly. Trucks arrive via an improvised dock; in the background an LST makes a delivery.

*A Fifteenth Air Force B-17, a portion of its wing shot away
by flak, falls toward Naples.*

the night of July 24/25 and began confusing the defenses of the city by
dropping strips of metal foil, called "window," which interfered with
electronic devices, particularly the antiaircraft tracking system called
Wurzburg. Great formations of British heavy bombers proceeded over
the city releasing quantities of high explosive and incendiary bombs.
Fires which quickly overwhelmed the Hamburg fire-fighting teams soon
covered the central city, serving as a seething beacon for Eighth Air
Force's bombers, which appeared the next day to concentrate on the
dock areas with especial attention to U-boat installations. The city was
still aflame when the British, having skipped a night, arrived over Hamburg with heavy bombers to stir the conflagration further. And so it continued with four attacks by the RAF and three by the Eighth Air Force.

The Germans called it a "catastrophe," and it was. Uncontrollable
fires linked to form a sea of flame resulting in the war's first "fire storm."

Air temperatures reached a thousand degrees and the vacuum produced by this heated air engulfed everything.

While there was a tragically heavy civil toll, heavy damage was done to industrial targets and the dock area. The cost in human lives ranges from 30,000 to 50,000—so many victims merely became ash that an accurate count was impossible. Close to 300,000 dwellings had been wiped out, leaving about 900,000 homeless in the Reich's second-largest city. Over 6,000 acres lay in ruins after the last flame was finally extinguished.

After North African airfields had been secured, it was possible for the Americans to begin operations from the south even before the Fifteenth Air Force was established at Foggia. During the Sicilian fighting two critical missions were flown from Africa. On July 19, 1943, General Doolittle, commander of the Twelfth Air Force, led more than 500 aircraft in an unprecedented mission to Rome—the objective: the two large railroad marshaling yards in the suburbs of the city.

The railway yards at San Lorenzo and Littorio were greatly damaged by the heavy bombers, while the medium bombers struck airfields in the area (of the 500 aircraft participating in the mission only two of the medium bombers were lost). Workshops, factories, tracks, and various vehicles were severely hit, but despite the careful planning, bomb spillage caused some damage to a basilica in the San Lorenzo area. However, no other religious buildings were hit.

During the Sicilian campaign a second American bombing mission was mounted from North African bases against the important Nazi-held Ploesti oil fields in Rumania. While this was in keeping with the high priority of oil targets in the Combined Bomber Offensive plan, it was also a gesture to the Russians, who had also been striking at Ploesti, the major source of German fuel and oil required on the Eastern Front.

Unlike the Rome mission, the Ploesti strike did not proceed as planned. After weeks of planning and training, 177 Liberator bombers took off from their North African bases shortly after dawn on August 1, 1943. The first mishap occurred over the Mediterranean when, inexplicably, the B-24 carrying the mission's lead navigator dropped into the sea.

Brigadier General Uzal G. Ent, in command of the mission, did not have full confidence in the young replacement navigator and, during the low-level approach to the target area, rejected the navigator's heading and led a number of aircraft into a wrong turn. By the time this error was detected and Ent switched course and led those planes that had followed him back toward Ploesti, the German-Rumanian defenses were ready for them.

Giant aircraft flying at only about 500 feet seemed to converge on the various targets from all directions. German antiaircraft guns, some

B-24 Liberators, at very low level, approach their targets at Ploesti, Rumania—the critical oil fields that supplied the Nazi war machine.

mounted on railway cars in the oil fields, fired point-blank at the Liberators and fighter planes swarming in from above. Ploesti churned with the bursting of bombs, the detonation of oil in storage tanks, and the crash of stricken bombers, some of them flying below chimney-stack height. Some pilots flew their planes through clouds of smoke and flame—many did not emerge.

While 42 per cent of Ploesti's refining capacity was knocked out and various other production sources were curtailed for several months, the Ploesti mission was not a success.

Fifty-four bombers were lost (and more than 500 men), a high ratio of loss for a single mission. It would be some time before the American bombers returned to Ploesti. Also, the rapidity with which the Germans were able to repair the damage, or switch to other plants for needed fuels, raised some doubts about the wisdom of attacking heavily defended oil targets.

Sixteen days after the ill-fated Ploesti mission the Eighth Air Force mounted a unique double mission from Britain. The targets were ball-bearing works at Schweinfurt and the Messerschmitt aircraft factory at Regensburg. The mission would be the deepest American penetration into Germany in fact, the flight to Regensburg was so distant that, instead

181

of turning around for the return to England, the Flying Fortresses were to continue on to North Africa.

On August 17 the double mission was flown, but not "as briefed." Rather typical English weather disrupted the schedule so that the Schweinfurt force took off some three hours, rather than ten minutes, after the Regensburg-North African force. No fighter plane then existed that could escort the bombers to and from targets inside Germany so that the German fighters waited until the Allied Thunderbolts (P-47s) and Spitfires, low on fuel, were forced to return to their bases.

The Luftwaffe met the American bombers in force and with every possible technique, from conventional fighter attacks to the use of rockets and parachute bombs. The Schweinfurt groups suffered this attention twice during the mission, to and from the target; the fact that the Regensburg bombers continued on to North Africa did confuse the German fighter commanders. Even so, the combined losses for the double mission was 60 Flying Fortresses out of the 376 dispatched—a disastrous loss rate.

The bombing had been generally good, especially at Regensburg, and production at both locations was disrupted or curtailed. One effect this had was to force the Germans to disperse their war industries and to seek certain materials elsewhere ("neutral" Sweden and Switzerland supplied ball bearings).

The year 1943 was one of bloodletting, of battles that yielded, in the phrase of Walt Whitman, "deeds of carnage." Brave deeds they were— but they created wasteful, inconclusive carnage.

Consider the Aleutian battleground in the northern Pacific and, in American eyes, so threatening of an invasion of the United States itself. The Japanese were established in the western end of the chain, at Kiska and Attu, but the Americans held the eastern end. On May 11, 1943, bypassing the more strongly held Kiska, the untested American 7th Infantry Division landed on Attu after heavy bombardment from the air and the sea. Though outnumbered the Japanese fought ferociously and the fighting did not stop, three weeks later, until the entire Japanese garrison was wiped out.

The costly lesson learned, the Americans dropped tons of bombs on Kiska (weather permitting) and a larger force was organized for the assault. On August 15, Canadian and American troops moved apprehensively over the muddy beaches of Kiska and found—no one. Some 5,000 Japanese troops had slipped away under the cover of the Aleutian fog.

In the Southwest and Central Pacific the Allies were ready in 1943 to go over to the offensive. MacArthur's forces moved up along the north coast of New Guinea from Buna toward the Huon Peninsula; Admiral William F. Halsey's forces moved upward from Guadalcanal in the

The light cruiser Nashville *turns off Kiska in the Aleutians, adding the weight of its firepower to the preassault barrage.*

Solomon Islands toward Bougainville. American air superiority, under the capable direction of feisty Lieutenant General George C. Kenney, greatly interfered with Japanese troop movements. In March he unleashed his Fifth Air Force against a 16-ship Japanese convoy on the way from Rabaul, New Britian, to Lae, on the Huon Peninsula, New Guinea. Intercepting the convoy in the Bismarck Sea, Kenney's airmen sank 12 ships (all of them troop transports).

Rabaul was the major objective of the movement up the spine of New Guinea and through the lush pestilence of the Solomons. It was the major Japanese sea and air base in the Southwest Pacific.

On June 30, MacArthur and Halsey began moving toward Rabaul with the virtually unopposed occupation of the Trobriand Islands, the invasion of Nassau Bay, New Guinea, and, in the Solomons, landings on Rendova Island, New Guinea, by U. S. Marine and Army troops. On August 7, Munda, New Georgia, was taken; the Allies owned another fine air base. The fighting in New Georgia was vicious, and the American forces suffered heavy casualties before the Japanese began evacuating New Georgia late in August (a process that was not complete until November).

In New Guinea, MacArthur's U.S. troops had invaded Nassau Bay from the sea while Australians closed in on Huon from the interior. A spectacular paratroop drop assured the construction of an airfield near Nadzab; the Australians took Finschhafen—by October 2, MacArthur's

183

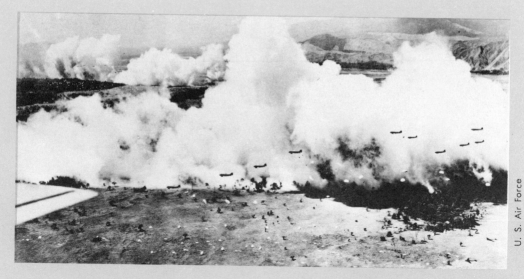

Airborne invasion: MacArthur's 503rd Parachute Infantry arriving at Nadzab, near Lae, New Guinea, behind a screen of smoke. Australian troops co-ordinated a ground attack with the jump and secured the area against the Japanese.

Rabaul, the great Japanese air and sea base, lay at the opposite end of New Britain from Cape Gloucester. Fifth Air Force bombers and fighters regularly attacked Rabaul, dropping 100-pound incendiary bombs to great effect against Japanese aircraft.

In the Central Pacific the Navy began a systematic harassment of Japanese-held islands. Carrier planes have just bombed and strafed Wake Island, which had fallen to the Japanese on December 23, 1941.

forces were established in the Huon Peninsula within reasonable distance, as the bomber flies, from Rabaul and just across the Vitiaz Strait from Cape Gloucester, New Britain.

One more major move was required to close out the Solomons campaign, the occupation of Bougainville. The assault began on November 1, 1943; the occupation could not begin until a week later. The Marines and Army troops encountered the usual tropical mud, jungle, and savagely fighting Japanese. The first day they held a beachhead some 600 yards wide—but still on the beach. From Rabaul came Japanese fighters and bombers to harry the Americans.

The comparative calm of the Central Pacific was shattered with landings in the Gilbert Islands, Makin and Tarawa, on November 20. Makin fell easily, but Tarawa was another story.

The Japanese had moved into the Gilbert Islands soon after Pearl Harbor and immediately fortified Betio, a tiny dot on the V-shaped atoll Tarawa, and proceeded to construct an airfield. From that little point in the Pacific, and others, the Japanese could strike at Allied shipping destined for Australia, New Guinea, or the Solomons. Betio Island was protected by a natural barrier reef, which compounded the risks of an amphibious assault; also the Japanese were well gunned and dug into ingeniously designed emplacements of coconut logs, coral, and sand. Networks of pillboxes lined the beaches.

185

President Roosevelt accompanied by General Eisenhower en route to Teheran for conferences with Churchill and Stalin, November–December 1943.

At dawn some 3,000 tons of explosives, from ships and the air, pounded the beaches of Betio. Two battalions of the 2nd Marine Division and one of the 8th churned ashore in amphibious tractors, followed by reinforcements in smaller landing craft. The first waves took a shallow beachhead, with light casualties, and were joined by others who were forced to wade through 500 yards of fire-swept water; casualties were heavy. At the end of the first day, the outcome was in doubt. Obviously, despite the heavy preinvasion bombardment, the Japanese had been so well dug in that the effect was minimal. Carrier aircraft and battleships with 16-inch guns poured more fire into the Japanese positions.

Ashore, the Marines fought desperately against a tough, death-oriented enemy with everything—tanks, mortars, rifles, grenades, and flame-throwers—and took, literally, an inch at a time. After three days —"76 stark and bitter hours" in the words of the Marine commander Major General Julian C. Smith—organized Japanese resistance at

186

Tarawa ended because virtually all of its garrison of 4,836 had been wiped out (4,690 killed) at great cost to the Marines—3,301 killed, missing, or wounded (over a thousand dead).

Tarawa had proved the efficacy of the amphibious assault on a heavily fortified atoll. It also confirmed the fanaticism of the Japanese soldier who preferred death to captivity; suicidal *banzai* attacks in the night, as the fighting came to a close, resulted in pointless casualties. The few prisoners were sullen and the Marines learned early that a Japanese prisoner was a willing walking booby trap, wired to explode when approached by his captors.

Tarawa taught another lesson: it could be wasteful to attempt to take every island in the Pacific occupied and fortified by the Japanese. It went down in the history of the Marine Corps as "Bloody Tarawa."

With Tarawa and Makin taken, the Central Pacific forces, under the command of Admiral Chester Nimitz, prepared for the next rung up the ladder, the Marshall Islands—and beyond: the Marianas, the Volcano Islands, whose Iwo Jima lay practically at Japan's doorstep.

During the height of the Tarawa battle a "Big Three" conference took place at Cairo, bringing together Roosevelt, Churchill, and China's Chiang Kai-shek. The emphasis was on the Pacific theater, with special attention given to yet another forgotten war front in the Far East, China-Burma-India. Burma was the key to China's supply lifeline and Burma was in Japanese control. Heading the newly established Southeast Asia Command was Admiral Lord Louis Mountbatten; his deputy was Lieutenant General Joseph W. Stilwell, who was also Chiang's chief of staff as well as commander in chief of all American forces in the CBI. Stilwell, who contemptuously referred to Chiang as "The Peanut" and was not on good terms with the Chinese leader (who was in fact stubborn, unco-operative, and demanding), had earned the nickname of "Vinegar Joe." Forced to fight with little in the way of supplies, troops, and top level understanding, he became a bitter critic of one and all.

Following the Cairo conference it was decided that the British would begin working back into Burma at the western frontier and Stilwell, commanding Chinese troops and with help from special units, Major General Orde C. Wingate's "Chindits" (a small airborne unit) and Major General Frank D. Merrill's "Marauders" (an American commando-like unit), would operate in northern Burma. The campaign opened on December 21.

Another "Big Three" conference took place on November 28 at Teheran, Iran, the first such conference in which Stalin participated. He promised that as soon as Germany was defeated the U.S.S.R. would declare war on Japan (it did not quite work out that way: Russia declared war on Japan when it was obvious that Japan was defeated). Churchill and Roosevelt promised a second European front in June 1944.

Russian women served on all fronts—and in the air; hero fighter pilot Lily Litvak on the wing of her Yak-9. She was killed in the fighting over the Eastern Front.

"Uncle Joe," as he was irreverently called by Roosevelt and Churchill, returned to Russia for the opening of the winter offensive. After the Stalingrad debacle, the Germans had been unable to mount a counteroffensive until March 1943 and had stopped the Russian advance, even succeeding in retaking Rostov and Kharkov. Army Group South, under Manstein, held a line along the Donets River from Rostov-on-Don to Belgorod. Opposite its left flank, and facing Army Group Center (Kluge), the line revealed an unsightly bulge, a chunky penetration into German-held territory just west of the city of Kursk. The line running north remained reasonably stable.

Hitler eyed the Kursk salient and demanded "one more victory that will shine like a beacon around the world." What he got was "Operation Citadel."

Operation Citadel was supposed to pinch the Kursk salient. Though planned for as early as March, Citadel was postponed by weather and Hitler's vacillations. On June 12 he ordered the operation to be executed. But the Russians, too, had been preparing. Since Barbarossa the Russians had learned their lessons well and developed tactics, training, leadership, and their own equipment (the new T-34 tank, for example, perhaps the most formidable tank of the war). An intangible element,

Russian troops on the move—and the Russian winter has set in; by year's end the Germans would be out of Russia.

and probably as deadly as all the rest, was the Russian desire to drive the Germans back to Berlin.

The two-pronged Citadel operation, the German Ninth Army in the north and the Fourth Panzer Army from the south, began on July 5. The Russian outer defenses fell before the heavy armor, particularly the Panther tanks. The Germans were on the move again and continued until July 9, although by the seventh Russian resistance had begun to stiffen. Great numbers of tanks on both sides were thrown into the battle, which evolved into the greatest armored battle of the war. On July 12 some 1,500 German and Russian tanks clashed at Prokhorovka, south of Kursk.

The Russian tanks broke through the German line of tanks and the machines jousted in a confused clash of metal and gunfire. When the battle ended in the evening, Operation Citadel was a failure and no less than 350 scorched German tanks covered the battleground. On July 13, Hitler called off Citadel.

But the Russians were not finished and opened an offensive north of the Kursk salient toward Bryansk and south of it toward Poltava. The Germans were obliged to hold until Hitler consented to their pulling back—and the holding cost heavily in German lives. Hitler, concerned with the way the war was proceeding in Sicily and then Italy, began moving troops out of the Russian front to the Mediterranean. Inexorably, the great Russian juggernaut moved westward, in wake of the retreating Wehrmacht. By the close of the year Soviet troops had pushed the Germans back across the Dnieper River at the southern end of the wide Russian front, taken back Kiev and Smolensk, and, in the north, even managed to get supplies into still-beleaguered Leningrad through a narrow corridor. Hitler talked of retaking Kiev, of reopening the Crimean front (by the winter of 1943 the Russians had reoccupied practically all of the economically valuable ground the Germans had taken). Hitler suspected that the Allies were preparing for a cross-Channel attack and in November he advised his generals in Russia that they would have to fend for themselves; he had important matters to consider in the West. When the wet winter came (it was not the usual hard freeze), some three million German troops, with few reserves, faced a massive Russian army of nearly six million equipped with great numbers of tanks and artillery.

On Christmas Eve the First Ukrainian Front smashed in the Fourth Panzer Army's front around Kiev; the broad front began moving west again. In November, when Manstein attempted another counteroffensive, Hitler promised commander General Hasso von Manteuffel, "As a Christmas present, I'll give you fifty tanks."

If, indeed, he kept his promise it did not alter the outcome. Christmas brought no joy to the Germans on the Eastern Front.

President Franklin D. Roosevelt shortly after arriving by plane at Rabat, Morocco, near Casablanca, for conferences with British Prime Minister Winston Churchill. The subjects: the plans for the invasions of Sicily and Italy and the return to France in 1944—and "unconditional surrender" of the Axis.

Casablanca, January 1943. Roosevelt, Churchill, and their military advisers (standing, left to right): Lieutenant General Henry H. Arnold (U. S. Army Air Forces), Admiral Ernest J. King (U. S. Navy), General George C. Marshall (U. S. Army), Admiral Sir Dudley Pound (Royal Navy), General Sir Alan Brooke (British Army), and Air Chief Marshal Sir Charles Portal (RAF).

Thorn in the side; Free French leader General Charles de Gaulle, who had hoped to have more to say at Casablanca than he was asked. Regarded by both Roosevelt and Churchill as troublesome, de Gaulle held a lifetime grudge against them for his treatment at Casablanca. A difficult ally, he united Frenchmen as did no other during the war.

While Eisenhower's troops moved eastward toward Tunisia, Montgomery moved from the south, pushing the Afrika Korps out of Libya. By January 23, the Eighth Army reached Tripoli; an Axis ammunition dump burns in the town abandoned by the Germans and Italians.

American paratroopers board a transport plane, North Africa. Although not widely used in the desert war, paratroopers attempted to secure a route to Tunis—in which race they were beaten by Rommel.

Another unit of Patton's "cavalry," an M-10 tank destroyer mounting a 3-inch gun; it was, in fact, a modified Sherman.

A destroyed panzer is out of the battle as a small Stuart passes by; this was the first American tank employed by the British in the war.

American troops advancing toward Tunisia across uncharacteristic desert terrain.

*British troops in a Churchill tank enter Tunis on the same
day the Americans took Bizerte.*

Stand-in for defeat: after Rommel, ailing and dispirited, left Tunisia, Colonel General Jurgen von Arnim was placed in command. On May 13 he surrendered all German forces in Tunisia, ending the war in Africa.

Overture to "Husky," the Allied amphibious-airborne assault on Sicily. Guns of the cruiser Boise *soften up the landing areas at Gela, the center of the American area of attack.*

Morning, July 10, 1943—landings on Sicily have begun and, with the coming of day, concern over the appearance of the Luftwaffe. The landing at Scoglitti, southeast of Gela, was virtually unopposed.

An Allied cargo ship, hit by an Axis dive bomber, smolders off the beaches of Sicily. A naval antiaircraft gun crew scans the sky for planes.

An LCM (Landing Craft, Mechanized), having delivered its cargo—120 men, or one medium tank, or 30 tons of supplies—plies the waters of Gela.

On the other side of the island, Montgomery's troops come ashore in the vicinity of Syracuse, Sicily. They had been preceded the night before by airborne troops whose operations were disrupted by poor weather.

The view from inside a landing craft onto the beach at Scoglitti, Sicily. These craft delivered men, vehicles, and supplies to the beachheads.

An amphibious "Duck" (DUKW, which letters meant it had been manu-
factured in the fourth year of the war [D], was a Utility craft, had four-
wheel drive [K], and the W meant it had six wheels for overland travel).
It was utilized for the first time in the Sicily invasion and proved to be a
most useful sea and land vehicle. It would be used later in the Pacific and in
the Normandy landings.

Wounded are taken aboard a ship for evacuation from the Sicilian coast.

Beachhead under contention, Salerno, Italy; Allied Intelligence learned that Italian troops had been moved out of the area and German units moved in. Counterattacks interfered with but did not stop the landings.

A British Spitfire with American markings after a reasonably smooth landing on the Palermo beach. Flying over beachheads was invariably hazardous to friend and foe alike.

By October, British and American forces, united, held about a third (the southern part) of Italy, which provided the Allies with air bases. This is an American night-fighter base near Grottaglie, Italy—the plane is a British Bristol Beaufighter, which was used by the U. S. Army Air Forces. Background smoke is a crash landing of a returning Beaufighter.

American Flying Fortresses bound for German targets. Without fighter escort the bomber formations suffered heavy losses during 1943.

British Short Stirling heavy bomber, one of the prime aircraft of Bomber Command in its night attacks on Germany.

Avro Lancaster warming up for a night mission. This was one of the outstanding aircraft of the war.

Lancaster over Hamburg, January 1943. Portions of the city are burning and flak patterns decorate the sky. In July, British bombers (night) and American bombers (day) struck Hamburg, causing a tremendous fire storm, the first of the war. Kassel, Berlin, Tokyo, and other cities would suffer similar calamities.

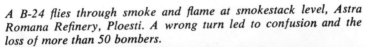

A B-24 flies through smoke and flame at smokestack level, Astra Romana Refinery, Ploesti. A wrong turn led to confusion and the loss of more than 50 bombers.

The remarkable De Havilland Mosquito, a fast, unarmed British bomber, reconnaissance aircraft (armed, it also tripled as a fighter). Constructed largely of wood, the Mosquito eluded radar detection and was one of the most efficient bombers of the war. Its speed, close to 400 mph., enabled the plane to attack its target before being detected and then outrun the Luftwaffe pursuers.

Schweinfurt, October 14, 1943. A B-17 heads for home leaving the target— the ball-bearing complex—smoking. Sixty Fortresses were lost on the costly mission, proving that daylight bomber assaults deep inside Germany required fighter escorts to fend off the determined German fighter pilots.

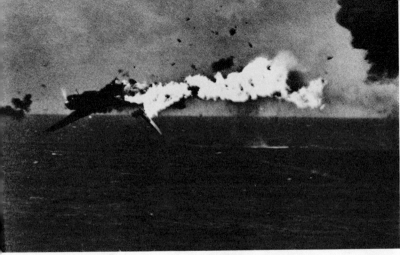

Moving northward from the Gilbert Islands, the Navy began preparing their next objectives, Roi and Kwajalein, in the Marshall Islands, with carrier-plane raids. Gunners of the Yorktown *have just flamed a Japanese torpedo bomber, a "Kate," off Kwajalein.*

Pounding the beaches of Kiska for the Canadian-American team. Upon landing, the troops found that the Japanese had abandoned their last position on the North American Continent.

Marines of the 1st Division wading ashore at Cape Gloucester, New Britain, last of New Guinea, to secure MacArthur's flank for the invasion of Hollandia.

Heinz J. Nowarra

The interminable war in Russia continues. Russian slave laborers bomb-up a German He-111 for yet another mission against unending targets.

Soviloto

Young Siberian soldier; fresh, determined, and tough—practically untouched by the war—would help drive the Germans out of Russia and back to Berlin.

The National Archives

Young German soldier on the Russian Front, the strain of battle obvious. He had little to look forward to but the approaching Russian winter.

A German artillery observer scans the Russian Front, summer 1943.

The National Archives

Better led and equipped than when Hitler first unleashed Barbarossa, Russian troops began counterattacks in September. Russian troops moving through farmland on the Desna River push the Germans back toward Smolensk.

Russian T-34 tanks, probably the most formidable tank of World War II, move against German positions. Panzers vs. T-34s resulted in tremendous tank battles such as that at Kursk, which stopped Hitler's Operation Citadel.

Russian fighters, the Yakolov Yak-9, which appeared in 1942, were most effective against German planes and tanks.

Lend-Lease: a Russian pilot (right, with chute) signs for an American A-20 light bomber, several thousand of which were delivered to the Soviets through this base at Abadan, Iran.

1944

To Free a Suffering Humanity

THE GREAT military achievement of 1944 was the Allied invasion of Normandy on the northwestern coast of France, the plans for which were put in motion by the Allies in January with the appointment of Eisenhower as Supreme Commander and a high-level staff of British and American leaders. Arriving in Britain on January 16, Eisenhower held his first conference on the twenty-first; his organization was known as Supreme Headquarters, Allied Expeditionary Force (SHAEF).

January was an active month on all fronts. On the eleventh the Russian Army crossed into Poland; in Italy, the Allies were blocked by the heavily fortified Gustav Line south of Rome, so Churchill suggested an alternative to Alexander, in full command in Italy since Eisenhower's departure. Landing craft, which were slated for the invasion in Southern France (to draw the Germans away from the north), were "borrowed" for a landing on the eastern coast of Italy behind the Gustav Line—and, lo! the road to Rome would be open. This task was assigned to the U. S. VI Corps under Major General John P. Lucas; under his command also were British infantry, armored units, and commandos. The assault, which did surprise the Germans but not for long, took place at Anzio on January 22. The Allies moved inland about ten miles, forming a pocket with their backs to the sea, and were stopped by strong German resistance, although the Anzio beachhead held.

A sore spot on the Gustav Line was Monte Cassino, on the pinnacle of which stood a 400-year-old Benedictine abbey. The Allies, certain that the Germans used the abbey as an observation post—with a magnificent overview of Allied positions to the south—began, with some reluctance but even greater fury, to bombard the abbey. The Germans insisted, and do to this day, that they did not use the abbey militarily.

Whatever the truth, the Allies believed that the abbey was occupied

Anzio beachhead, January 22, 1944, the Allied attempt to get around the Gustav Line, which stood in the way of the drive to Rome.

by Germans and proceeded to destroy it by artillery fire and aerial bombardment. Despite such saturation bombing, efforts by various Allied troops, New Zealand, British, American, and Indian, Monte Cassino would not yield. Part of the problem was the solution: the heavy bombardment filled the streets with rubble, making progress difficult or impossible for troops and vehicles. After regrouping, the Allies attempted striking at the Gustav Line in May, finally taking the abbey on May 18. The line moved upward in Italy and the Allies who had been entrapped in Anzio broke out under the leadership of General Mark Clark. On May 25, Clark's Fifth Army linked with Alexander's units moving through the Gustav Line. The race for Rome was on—the triumphant entry into a capital city was one of the peripheral, not very productive, obsessions of military men. Clark reached Rome first, on June 4, but at the same time German troops managed to slip away to dig in in the north. The entry of Rome did not end the fighting in Italy.

In January the Russians could announce yet another victory: on January 27 the long-suffering "Hero City," Leningrad, was relieved at last.

On January 29 in the Pacific, Nimitz began the sequel to the taking of the Gilberts, the campaign in the Marshall Islands, with carrier strikes

EUROPE
1944

Pre-war Frontiers

ATLANTIC
OCEAN

SWEDEN

FINLAND

NORWAY

Oslo

Helsinki

Leningrad

U.S.S.R.

Stockholm

ESTONIA

NORTH SEA

DENMARK

BALTIC
SEA

LATVIA

LITHUANIA

ELAND

LAND

ENGLAND

NETHERLAND

London

Antwerp   *Arnhem*
Dover   *Calais*   *Nijmegen*
BELGIUM   *Eindhoven*
Aachen

OVERLORD
JUNE 6/44

LUX.

ENTIN PEN.
St. Lo

CAN. IST ARMY
BR. 2ND ARMY

Bastogne

BATTLE OF
THE BULGE

Paris   *Metz*
Falaise
U.S. IST ARMY

ELBE R.

Berlin

GERMANY

VISTULA R.

Warsaw

EAST
PRUSSIA

POLAND

Prague

CZECHOSLOVAKIA

RHINE R.

DANUBE R.

U.S. 3RD
ARMY

SEINE R.

MEUSE R.

LOIRE R.

FRANCE

SWITZ.

Vichy

U.S. 6TH
ARMY

FR. IST
ARMY

BAY OF
BISCAY

RHONE R.

AUSTRIA

Vienna

Budapest

HUNGARY

ROMANIA

Ploesti

Bucharest

ITALY

PO   R.

Florence   *Rimini*

Belgrade

DANUBE R.

YUGOSLAVIA

BULGARIA

Sofia

Marseilles   *St. Tropez*
Toulon   AUG.
15/44

SPAIN

CORSICA

Rome
Anzio   *Monte
Cassino*

JAN. 22/44

ADRIATIC
SEA

ALBANIA

GREECE

AEGEAN
SEA

SARDINIA

Athens

MEDITERRANEAN SEA

SICILY

CRETE

ALGERIA   TUNISIA

0   Miles   300
0   Km.   300

PACIFIC THEATER
1944

PACIFIC OCEAN

MARSHALL IS.
GILBERT IS.

WAKE

ENIWETOK
FEB.17

KWAJALEIN
JAN.31

SAIPAN JUNE 15
TINIAN JULY 24

GUAM JULY 21

CAROLINE IS.

BATTLE OF
PHILIPPINE SEA
JUNE 19-20

✕

PALAU
SEPT.15

SOLOMON IS.

Rabaul

Finschhafen
JAN.2

Port
Moresby

NEW GUINEA

APR.22

WAKDE
MAY 17

Hollandia

MOROTAI
SEPT.15

Sansapor
JULY 30

VOGELKOP PEN.

Darwin

AUSTRALIA

DUTCH EAST INDIES

BORNEO

BATTLE OF
LEYTE GULF
OCT. 24-26

HALSEY
SPRAGUE
KINKAID

SAN
BERNARDINO
STRAIT

SURIGAO
STRAIT

MINDANAO

SHIMA

NISHIMURA

KURITA

OZAWA

C. ENGAÑO

LUZON

Manila

SIBUYAN
SEA

PHILIPPINE IS.

LEYTE
OCT. 20

TAIWAN

Hongkong

Hankow

C   H   I   N   A

Yenan

Sian

Chungking

YELLOW

YANGTZE

Kunming

BURMA ROAD

LEDO ROAD

Ledo
Myitkyina

Kohima
Imphal
INDIA

BURMA

Rangoon

THAILAND

Hanoi

INDOCHINA

MALAYA

Singapore

SUMATRA

Batavia

INDIAN OCEAN

KOREA

JAPAN

Tokyo

PACIFIC OCEAN

The long, deadly siege of Leningrad ended as 1944 began; German prisoners are herded into captivity by victorious Russian troops.

The Polish Corps finally took Monte Cassino, breaking the Gustav Line in May. Cassino was an utter ruin, making movement forward difficult. But the race for Rome was on.

and naval bombardment of Wotje, Taroa, Kwajalein, Roi-Namur, and other tiny points in the island group. The major objective was the island of Kwajalein at the southeast end of the pearl-like string of islands and islets of the Kwajalein Atoll; in the north lay Roi-Namur, two small islands joined by a causeway, and Kwajalein Island; both contained Japanese airfields. Once these were taken, the Japanese on other atolls and islets could be cut off from supplies and aid by sea and air power.

The lesson of Tarawa had been learned: preassault bombardment was heavier and prolonged. The first waves ashore would carry field artillery to be set up for ferreting out pinpoint targets such as deeply dug-in positions not susceptible to area saturation by big guns.

Following a period of heavy bombardment, and while other Japanese air bases in the Marshalls were kept closed by air strikes of Navy carrier planes and bombers of the Seventh Air Force, the invasion of Kwajalein opened on January 31, 1944. Kwajalein Island was assigned to the Army's 7th Infantry Division, veterans of the Aleutian campaign (and veterans of the weather gamut of the war); freshly arrived from the United States, the Marine 4th Division was to land at Roi-Namur.

Despite some confusion among the green Marines, Roi-Namur was secured within two days; Kwajalein took four, but the new approach had worked. At the cost of 174 killed and missing and 700 wounded the Marines and the Army took Kwajalein literally within a few days. Fifty Japanese prisoners were taken and 4,650 were dead, a number of them by suicide.

Eniwetok, some 285 miles to the west, was invaded on February 18 and, after fierce fighting by the stunned Japanese, fell by the twenty-second. Before the invasion was attempted, Task Force 58, of the U. S. Fifth Fleet, dispatched bombers to deal with Truk, in the Caroline Islands, west of the Gilberts and north of New Guinea. Truk had been a great Japanese naval base and a powerful nest of air power, but by February the bulk of the Japanese fleet had fled to less vulnerable waters to the west. Still Vice Admiral Marc Mitscher's planes and ships found much to work over. They left more than 250 Japanese planes scattered over Truk's bombed-out runways; dozens of ships of all types were sunk or destroyed in their docks. The attackers lost 25 aircraft, with 29 crewmen; the *Intrepid* was struck by a torpedo but was capable of returning to port. Truk as a great Japanese base was finished.

Meanwhile, in MacArthur's portion of the Pacific, Cape Gloucester in New Britain had been taken in December 1943 with the help of a few Marines. With his right flank secure, with Rabaul being regularly worked over by bombers, MacArthur could continue up the northern coast of New Guinea. At the end of February, American forces moved into the Admiralty Islands, to the north of New Guinea, and seized an airstrip on Los Negros. By April 22, after a heavy aerial bombardment,

Supreme Commander of the Normandy invasion, General Eisenhower visits a paratroop base in England. These men would jump into the invasion area the night before the amphibious assault began.

including naval planes of Task Force 58, MacArthur's troops made an unopposed landing at Hollandia, New Guinea, well up the back of the island.

In the European Theater, still the major area of concern, planning for "Operation Overlord" was being formulated under British Lieutenant General Frederick E. Morgan with the official designation of COSSAC (Chief of Staff to the Supreme Allied Commander).

The planning encompassed millions of details: men, machines, supplies, aircraft, ships, airborne troops, weather, the condition of the beaches—a stunning undertaking. To confuse German Intelligence, elaborate cloak-and-dagger schemes were devised. Patton was freed from durance vile in Sicily, where he had languished after his infamous "slapping incident," and was placed in command of the Third Army (which would not participate in the initial assault) and was encouraged to behave in a warlike manner in the general area of Dover in order to convince the Germans that the invasion would come at Calais.

Field Marshal Gerd von Rundstedt, Commander in Chief, West, was certain that Calais would be it. He was contradicted by Rommel, who had been transferred from Italy to the west. Agreeing with Rommel was Rundstedt's supreme leader, Hitler. His "intuition" told him that the Allies would land in Normandy—and he was right.

213

Rommel and Rundstedt disagreed on how the situation should be handled when it, inevitably, came. Rommel believed that the Allies should be destroyed on the sea and the shore. Commander in Chief, West, preferred letting the enemy come ashore and then annihilating them on land with troops and tank units waiting behind the beaches. Rommel, drawing on his African experience, worried about the fate of those reserves attempting to move up under Allied air superiority.

There were only intermittent stretches of fortified coastline—much of it the work of Rommel. Gun emplacements lined the coast, but these too were scattered and much of the vaunted Atlantic Wall, which Hitler boasted of but never saw, was uncompleted. By April, Rommel, ignoring Rundstedt as much as was militarily proper, pushed his troops to construct the beach defenses.

The only area on the coast of France fortified sufficiently to deserve being called the Atlantic Wall was at Pas-de-Calais. The Overlord planners had their eyes on the beaches of Normandy to the west. But so did Hitler and Rommel.

Meanwhile heavy air attacks were made on various target systems throughout France—not merely in and around Normandy. Transportation—roads, rails, bridges—in Northern France was repeatedly bombed. By this time both Hitler and Rommel revised their views and began thinking that the Allies planned a massive invasion and that Normandy would be only one, and secondary, phase of it. Consequently, the 58 German divisions of Rommel's Army Group B and Colonel General Johannes von Blaskowitz's Army Group G (in Southern France) were spread from the Netherlands, down the western coast of France, and eastward to the Italian frontier.

In May, when the Germans expected the invasion, Eisenhower set the date for June 5. With more than two million men, 5,000 ships and craft of all types, and more than 8,000 aircraft, bombers and fighter planes, poised for the June 5 landings, Eisenhower canceled them because of poor weather. On the fifth the weather had improved somewhat, but the water was still choppy in the Channel; further delay would mean an even longer postponement until the tides were favorable again. In that period the Germans might become more informed, and the keyed-up Allied troops less determined.

The lonely final decision was Eisenhower's; after weighing all factors he decided that the invasion was on. June 6, 1944, would be D-Day.

The great man-made machinery of men and armament sprang into motion with RAF bombers ranging through the invasion area bombing coastal batteries and other targets. Out of the night, in the west, American paratroopers dropped to earth; in the east a British airborne division did the same.

In the early hours before dawn thousands of landing craft headed for

British troops come ashore at Gold, Juno, and Sword Beaches, to the east of Omaha. On Gold the men were pinned down for a while, but by the end of the day had advanced five miles inland.

Normandy, June 6, 1944. With barrage balloons overhead (a precaution against Luftwaffe incursion—which did not occur) men and supplies pour ashore. The Allies have come to France to stay.

the beaches. The U. S. First Army (Lieutenant General Omar Bradley) on the western end at Utah and Omaha Beaches; the British Second Army (Lieutenant General Sir Miles C. Dempsey) came in at the center and at the eastern end of the invasion area, at Gold, Juno, and Sword Beaches.

Despite some mishaps (paratroopers dropped in the wrong area, landing in trees or drowning in swamps) and hard fighting, especially on "bloody" Omaha Beach, Overlord was an overwhelming success; the Allies had opened up a second front and they had come to France to stay.

Eisenhower announced the landings once the secret was out; he was followed later in the day by Roosevelt's prayer: "Our sons, pride of our nation, this day have set upon a mighty endeavor, a struggle to preserve our Republic, our religion and our civilization and to set free a suffering humanity . . ." Joining the Americans in this mighty endeavor were also the pride of Britain and Canada—and French resistance fighters striking out of the dark. By nightfall of what Rommel (who had been on leave in Germany on D-Day) called "the longest day," tens of thousands of Allied troops, tons of supplies, and thousands of vehicles had come ashore. Three weeks later nearly a million men had arrived along with 177,000 vehicles and 500,000 tons of supplies; the opportunity to push them back into the sea was gone.

Hitler urged his commanders to hold on, promising the introduction of "secret weapons" that would decide the outcome of the war. On June 13 the first of the German "Vengeance" weapons, a V-1 rocket missile, landed in England. While frightening, these flying bombs were hardly noted for their pinpoint accuracy; even so, their random terrorism was a cause for concern in the Allied camp. By July 6, Churchill announced that the V-1s had killed 2,752 people, most of them civilians. Allied bombers had been attacking the launching sites for some time but with little result, for the emplacements were hard to find and even more difficult to damage. The speed of the V-1 and the later, more powerful wingless rocket the V-2, made them difficult to deal with in the air.

For the Allies fighting westward out of the landing areas, especially on the Cotentin Peninsula south of Cherbourg, was made difficult by the hedgerows that enclosed the farmland of the area. The earth and brush constructions, often lined with watery ditches, provided perfect defensive positions for the Germans. The American First Army, after heavy casualties, finally broke out of the hedgerow and by July 18 reached St. Lô. In the east the British, too, were held at Caen and were assisted by heavy air attacks toward Falaise.

The Allies continued to enjoy air supremacy over the battlefields, and the Germans found it difficult to move during the daytime over the roads. One victim of a strafing attack was Rommel, whose command car was shot up and driven into a ditch by a fighter plane. Suffering a brain concussion, Rommel left France, his career as a soldier over. Three days later an attempt by disgruntled German officers was made on Hitler's life, the abortive "Bomb Plot" of July 20. Among those implicated was Rommel, who chose to commit suicide rather than go through the process of a mock trial. Hitler struck back savagely and some 150 conspirators, many of doubtful guilt, were executed.

In Normandy, Rommel's command was taken over by Field Marshal Hans Guenther von Kluge—who had also taken over for von Rundstedt early in July. Kluge was thus both Commander in Chief as well as commanding officer of Army Group B. An able and outspoken officer, Kluge tended to tell Hitler the truth of what was happening in Normandy. Hitler did not wish to hear this; his distrust of generals and other High Command officials was evident. He recalled von Kluge in August, replacing him with General Walther Model. On his way back to Germany Kluge poisoned himself.

Late in July the Allies staged a real breakthrough under the direction of Bradley and with the aid of heavy bombardment. On August 1, Patton's Third Army became officially operational; a week later Eisenhower established his headquarters in France. Although the Germans managed a counteroffensive on August 7, the drive for Paris had begun. Montgomery, now in command of British forces in the north, began converging with Bradley's troops in the south. Spearheaded by Patton, the Allies drove the Germans back and by August 25 had reached the Seine River (north), the Loire River (south), and Paris.

The delayed "Operation Anvil" (the invasion of Southern France) was launched on August 15 against Blaskowitz's Army Group G. American and French troops came ashore in the St.-Tropez area practically unopposed. By September 15 advance patrols linked up with Patton's swiftly moving Third Army.

"The Hun is on the run" was the general feeling and there was a (premature) sense of victory in the air as Allied troops liberated more of France (including those near Calais and its V-1 launching sites), and entered Belgium and Holland. A near encirclement of two German armored divisions by Canadian and American troops had led to an almost disorganized German withdrawal so that by mid-September the U. S. First Army had reached the Siegfried Line—the West Wall—at Germany's frontier.

Plans were formulated for the final thrust into Germany, a double-pronged stab by Montgomery in the north (through the heart of the Ruhr's iron and steel complex) and by Patton in the south, toward Metz, which would threaten the secondary industrial area, the Saar basin. Lieutenant General Courtney H. Hodges' First Army would move forward between the Montgomery-Patton arrows.

The National Archives

A German spy is executed by an American firing squad, France, 1944.

Free French troops, in American battle clothes, move through a village on the road to Paris.

French Embassy Press Division

Montgomery managed to add a brilliant touch to the advance of the Allies. To smash across the barrier of the Rhine River in the north and possibly outflank the West Wall, he proposed the dropping of three airborne divisions in Holland behind the lines to disrupt German defenses while the British Second Army surged ahead across the Rhine and toward the Ruhr. The first phase, the drop of British and American paratroopers, was code-named "Market"; the last phase, "Garden," the invasion of the Ruhr, never came off.

The airborne invasion was successful as British and American paratroopers floated unexpectedly down in the area of Arnhem, Nijmegen, and Eindhoven on September 17. Though surprised, the Germans happened to have two panzer divisions in the area. They were thrown in against the advancing Allies. By September 25, Garden was called off and the survivors of Market (some 2,000 of nearly 9,000) withdrew from the north bank of the Rhine.

Doubts began to arise as to the quick ending of the war. Hitler had sent Rundstedt back to the Western Front, where he stiffened the lines along the Dutch-Belgian border, the West Wall, and in Northeastern France, along the Moselle River. The Allies' rapid advance had introduced the usual problem of extended supply lines—forward troops were often 500 miles from their depots. Despite the 24-hour-a-day operations of the famous Red Ball Express, armored units often ran out of fuel and were stopped in their tracks. Winter weather, too, bogged down the forward advance.

When the supply situation improved somewhat, in early November, Eisenhower ordered a new offensive by the First Army toward Aachen. In the north this was assisted by Lieutenant General William Simpson's U. S. Ninth Army and in the south by Patton's Third. The plan was to establish positions and bridgeheads from which to launch a major offensive into Germany after the new year.

By the middle of 1944 there were enough fronts to satisfy Stalin: a double-pronged front moving across France, another moving northward from Rome in Italy. On Stalin's own front, Hitler was faring badly also. Opposite Germany's Army Group Center, where the Russians were not expected to attack, the Russians began the summer offensive on June 22. Expecting the blow in the north, Hitler had 80 per cent of Army Group Center's tanks transferred to Army Group North Ukraine. Consequently when the commanders on the scene suggested intelligent withdrawal, Hitler refused to accept that. Within two weeks Army Group North lost 25 of its 38 divisions. By July the Russian thrust split into two forces: the northern flank created a corridor between Army Group North and Army Group Center and rolled on toward East Prussia and the Baltic. The southern flank reached the suburbs of Warsaw by July 31.

Luftwaffe gun-camera film. A German fighter pilot approaches a B-17 from behind, sets the left outboard engine afire, and dives below the belly turret (with two projecting machine guns; the guns of the chin turret point down and to the right).

On other parts of the Russian Front, opposite Army Group South Ukraine, the Russians pushed through Rumania, which declared war on Germany shortly after surrendering to the Russians. The same occurred with Bulgaria, invaded shortly after Russian troops secured the Ploesti oil fields in Rumania. Hungary proved to be a tougher adversary, primarily because it was occupied by German troops. But on December 29, Hungary surrendered and declared war on Germany.

On the Russian northern front, the Russians eliminated the Finns from the war when an offensive into the Karelian Isthmus was opened on June 9, 1944. The Finns were driven back to the 1940 Russian-Finnish border and in September signed an armistice.

On the Italian front, Alexander's forces were drained to some extent (seven divisions) for participation in the invasion of Southern France. Despite this, Alexander began moving up the Italian peninsula on August 25 and by the end of September had succeeded in breaking through the heavily fortified Gothic Line. An Allied line, some 150 miles long,

U. S. Air Force

*Target: Berlin. The German capital under aerial attack in
this Air Force strike photo. Berlin was the most bombed
city in Germany.*

ran across Italy from east to west north of Rimini and Florence. But
movement in Italy was slow and casualties high. The autumn rains, then
as before, fell and bogged down extended advances, leaving the Allies
hungrily in sight of the Po Valley.

During February, the so-called "Big Week" (from the nineteenth
through the twenty-fifth), the RAF and the two American strategic air
forces, the Eighth and the Fifteenth, collaborated on missions aimed
particularly at Luftwaffe targets by night and day. The ironic paradox of
this kind of campaign was that the more the Allies attacked German aircraft targets, the greater German aircraft production seemed to increase.
This was accomplished partly because of the difficulty of destroying such
targets and because, when the Germans realized they were slated for systematic attacks, they dispersed the factories.

Despite the increase of production, under the direction of Hitler's
protégé, Albert Speer, the Luftwaffe was seriously crippled by Allied
air superiority and the loss of experienced fighter pilots in the great air
battles.

The Allied tactical air units, the light and medium bombers and
fighters, after D-Day could operate from fields in France to harry the
German troops, vehicles, and tanks. A very effective system of dealing
with German panzers evolved using an observer with a radio in contact
with fighter-bombers, of which the Thunderbolt was one of the most
effective.

Allied air superiority was so overwhelming that by the end of August

221

Southwest Pacific top brass: in Brisbane, Australia, are Gerard Forde, F. M. Forde, Australian Minister for the Army, General Douglas MacArthur, General Sir Thomas Blamey, commander of the Australian Land Forces, and Lieutenant General Richard K. Sutherland, MacArthur's Chief of Staff.

RAF's Bomber Command had begun to abandon its nighttime area bombing to attack targets in the Ruhr during the day.

Air power was critical in the Pacific war also. The battleship of tradition was being supplanted by the carrier. With both Navy and Army Air Force assistance, MacArthur continued to leapfrog along the northern New Guinea coast despite hard-fought battles. By April the Allies had reached Hollandia in Netherlands New Guinea, then moved up to Wakde Island and, by the end of July, reached Sansapor on the Vogelkop Peninsula at the northeastern end of New Guinea. On September 15 tiny Morotai Island, in the Molucca Islands—and just southeast of the Philippines—was in American hands.

In the Central Pacific the U. S. Fifth Fleet, under Admiral Raymond A. Spruance, and amphibious forces, under Vice Admiral Richard K. Turner, struck at Saipan in the Mariana Islands on June 15. Saipan was less than 1,500 miles from Tokyo and the heart of the Marianas' defenses. Some 30,000 Japanese Army and Imperial Marine troops fought the Marine assault bitterly.

Combined Fleet Commander Admiral Soemu Toyoda, upon learning of the attack in the Marianas, ordered his ships and carrier force to positions to the east of the Philippines. Task Force 58, Mitscher's carriers,

Action in the Central Pacific: a Hellcat takes off from a carrier deck during an early hit-and-run raid on Saipan, Mariana Islands.

Marines come ashore at Saipan, June 15, 1944. Fighting was bitter, for the Japanese were determined to hold this important base in the Marianas.

moved toward the enemy ships that had been reported by U.S. submarines. Japanese carrier planes launched the first attack in the morning of June 19, beginning the Battle of the Philippine Sea, better known as the "Marianas Turkey Shoot." At a cost of 26 American Navy pilots, the Japanese lost more than 200 planes and crews; in addition, American submarines sank two carriers, the *Taiho* and *Shokaku*. On the twentieth, Mitscher's TF 58 began pursuing the retreating Japanese fleet, sank sev-

223

"Marianas Turkey Shoot." American landings on Saipan brought a strong Japanese naval reaction on June 19. Met by U.S. naval planes, the attacking aircraft were shot down wholesale. A falling Japanese bomber just misses the Kitkun Bay.

eral small ships and the carrier *Hiyo;* two other carriers, the *Zuikaku* and *Chiyoda,* were seriously damaged.

On Saipan the fighting continued until July 9 as men of the 2nd and 4th Marine Divisions and the Army's 27th Division wiped out the Japanese defense force (some 30,000 men). American dead numbered 3,000. Other important islands in the Marianas were more easily secured. The way to the Philippines was now open.

The invasion of the Philippines was set for December 10, but on the advice of Admiral Halsey, who noted the weak opposition to his carrier plane attacks in the Philippines, the date was set ahead two months. Hard fighting faced the Americans who had come with MacArthur as desperate Japanese dug in, ready to die where they were. The fighting, costly to both Americans and Japanese, was not decided until the begin-

224

American landings in the Philippines on October 20, 1944, triggered the second Battle of the Philippine Sea (the first was the Marianas Turkey Shoot), better known as the Battle for Leyte Gulf. Three large Japanese naval forces attempted to destroy the American fleet around the Philippines. A Japanese kamikaze has just hit a carrier deck.

ning of the new year, when, except for some mopping up, Japanese resistance flickered out.

During the land battle on Leyte, the greatest naval battle of the war was fought, the Battle for Leyte Gulf. The loss of the Philippines meant also the loss of an important fuel source so Admiral Toyoda risked what remained of his fleet after the Marianas debacle to deny the Americans the Philippines and to turn the invasion into an American disaster. It was a gamble that almost paid off.

Toyoda had devised a complex plan: the decoying of Admiral William Halsey's Third Fleet away to the north from the Leyte invasion beaches. The Seventh Fleet, commanded by Vice Admiral Thomas C. Kinkaid, also covering the landings, had only a small escort carrier force.

From October 23 to 26 a series of overlapping sea-air battles flared around Leyte Gulf. While three Japanese attack forces approached from the west to swing around the Leyte beachhead from two directions, a fourth unit, Vice Admiral Jisaburo Ozawa's Northern Force with four virtually empty carriers, lured Halsey's carrier forces away from the scene. In the north, however, Halsey's Third Fleet came within reach of

Japanese land-based aircraft that succeeded in sinking one of his carriers, the *Princeton*.

American planes, meanwhile, had spotted Vice Admiral Takeo Kurita's Second Fleet in the Sibuyan Sea approaching Leyte from the north, and left the battleship *Musashi* sinking and several ships damaged, but Kurita persisted. Approaching from the south the "C" Force, under Vice Admiral Shoji Nishimura, was caught in the Surigao Strait between Leyte and Mindanao. As the Japanese ships attempted to pass through the strait in a neat file, American ships on either side opened up on them. Nishimura's force was torn to bits by the heavy guns of the Seventh Fleet. The flagship *Yamashiro* sank, taking Nishimura with it. Coming behind "C" Force was the Second Attack Force (Vice Admiral Kiyohide Shima), but too late to help Nishimura.

Kurita's force meanwhile had swung southward through San Bernardino Strait around Samar Island, toward Leyte Gulf. Caught off guard, the Seventh Fleet's small carrier force, under the command of Rear Admiral Clifton F. Sprague, fled to the cover of a rain squall after launching its planes and calling for help in plain English (there being no time for codes). The half-dozen or so vulnerable escort carriers and a few smaller ships were all that stood between Kurita's heavily gunned fleet and the beaches of Leyte.

Although he did not believe his ships "could survive another five minutes," Sprague ordered his few destroyers, destroyer escorts, and planes to attack Kurita's force. Dodging, turning, and hiding, the Americans fought back, convincing Kurita that he'd best get out of the reach of the American air strikes and away from the larger American forces. With his goal all but in sight, Kurita ordered his ships to withdraw, under pursuit by American carrier planes.

Halsey, who had been engaged in destroying Ozawa's helpless carrier force, attempted to race back to aid Sprague but arrived after Kurita's retreat. American carrier planes had sent all four Japanese carriers to the bottom. The Battle for Leyte Gulf had cost the Japanese Navy 26 fighting ships and the Americans six, but it had been a near thing.

During the Leyte Gulf battles a new weapon of despair was introduced by the Japanese, *kamikaze*. Deliberate suicide attacks were made on ships of the Seventh Fleet by Japanese pilots whose planes carried heavy explosive loads. One small carrier was sunk, but the kamikaze attacks were more destructive than decisive, causing damage to ships (carriers were a favorite target) and killing and horribly maiming crews.

In the lesser known area of the east, the China-Burma-India Theater, the war against the Japanese accelerated in 1944, with special emphasis, in Burma. With minimal co-operation from Chiang Kai-shek, the Allies began pushing the Japanese out of positions they had occupied since

CBI, the neglected theater: a group tours an Allied base in China. Lieutenant General Henry Arnold, U. S. Air Force; Brigadier General Claire L. Chennault, once commander of the Flying Tigers and later of the Fourteenth Air Force in China; Lieutenant General Joseph W. Stilwell, outspoken leader of American and Chinese troops in China-Burma-India; Field Marshal Sir John Dill, who served as liaison between British and Americans of the Joint Chiefs of Staff; and Brigadier General Clayton L. Bissell, later commander of the U. S. Tenth Air Force.

early in the war. British-Indian troops drove the Japanese out of the Kohima-Imphal area, India. Stilwell, aided more by Merrill's Marauders than by his own Chinese troops, took the Myitkyina, Burma, airfield by May 17. Aided by the famed Special Force (the former "Chindits"), Stilwell reopened the land route to China by taking the Ledo Road, the western section of the Burma Road.

The Japanese, spurred by the presence in Chinese bases of a new bomber, the Boeing B-29 Superfortress, took the initiative in China. From southern Chinese bases the B-29s of the Twentieth Air Force had begun bombing the Japanese homeland. Actually, B-29 operations out of China were not especially effective because of the distance, weather, and supply problems. The Japanese were not aware of this, only of the fact of an occasional B-29 bombing of Japan, and moved to occupy the airfields. By the end of the year Japanese troops, defeating the Chinese defenders, had taken all but two of the B-29 bases in China.

By the close of 1944, however, B-29s had begun operating against the Japanese homeland from strategically positioned Saipan, in the

227

American soldiers in the snowy Ardennes, startled by the unexpected German counterattack; the Battle of the Bulge has begun, December 16, 1944.

Marianas. From these tiny islands in the Central Pacific the 21st Bomber Command under Major General Curtis E. LeMay (who would assume command on January 20, 1945) incinerated several Japanese industrial-military cities, including Tokyo itself.

By early December 1944, American troops were solidly entrenched in the Philippines and on December 8 the U.S. air forces in the Pacific began bombarding another dot practically at Japan's doorstep, Iwo Jima.

In Europe the war took a bad turn for the Allies with the unleashing of a new Hitlerian brainstorm. He planned to close 1944 with a surprise counteroffensive that would stun and divide the Allies. Germany for the first time during the war went on a total wartime basis; the draft age was lowered to age sixteen and war production was increased, despite the Allied bombings. The German manpower barrel was scraped and, in the face of his military advisers' questionings, Hitler had 20 divisions, seven of them armored, sent to the Western Front. His plan: to drive a wedge

228

into the weakest sector of the Allied line—through the Ardennes Forest —cross the Meuse, and continue on to Antwerp, the critical Belgian port city. The Allies would be separated and the Germans would once again control the Western Front. Although he himself would be in command. Hitler brought Field Marshal von Rundstedt out of retirement to serve as nominal commander in chief of the operation, *Wacht am Rhein.*

On December 16, after several delays, following a massive artillery barrage, the panzers smashed into the Ardennes. Strung out along this line were some 80,000 generally unprepared and unsuspecting American troops. Rushing at them were 200,000 ready and able Germans under the spell of Hitler's plan.

The blow was struck across the Siegfried Line directly at that sector held by the American VIII Corps, which reeled back as the Germans poured into the large gap. Where the confused Americans held, an armored German task force would move in to wipe them out—the most notorious of these being *Kampfgruppe Peiper,* led by Lieutenant Colonel Jochen Peiper, whose drive penetrated 15 miles inside the American lines before he was stopped by American reserves and, when the

Clear skies, reinforcements, and supplies enabled the Allies to begin smoothing out the Bulge. Hitler's Wacht am Rhein *had failed.*

Culver Pictures

weather cleared, by the Thunderbolt fighter-bombers that mangled his tanks.

By Christmas a wedge-like penetration of about 60 miles deep had been made in the Allied line, the Battle of the Bulge had begun. Inside that bulge, in the town of Bastogne, Belgium, troops of the 101st Airborne Division stubbornly refused to surrender though surrounded. As for the Meuse, only an armored German spearhead had approached within three miles of the river before being wiped out by the U. S. 2nd Armored Division.

Weather had, for a time, served Hitler—the foggy Ardennes contributed to the confusion, grounded the fighter-bombers for a time, and interfered with dropping supplies to the men inside the Bulge. Allied reaction after the initial surprise had dissipated was quick. Eisenhower placed Montgomery in charge of the northern sector of the Bulge and Bradley the south. Reserves were fed in from both directions as soon as possible. The Germans were especially worried about their south flank, for Patton's Third Army began rushing to the aid of encircled Bastogne, which he reached on December 26.

The truth was that Hitler's *Wacht am Rhein* had run out of steam. The Americans had held, despite lesser numbers and disorganization. Swift redeployment of Allied troops, the clearing weather, and the usual supply problems that afflicted the Germans when they moved ahead quickly decided the issue.

Major General John P. Lucas, commander of the Anzio landings, and British General Sir Harold Alexander, Commander in Chief, Italy.

Evacuating the wounded at Anzio. Ten German divisions faced the four Allied divisions that took the Anzio beachhead. Although the Allies held it, months would pass before Rome would be reached—and many more casualties.

British troops, covered by comrades in a shell hole, move through the rubble of an Italian town.

A few of the handful of Japanese prisoners taken at Kwajalein. Stripping them was a necessary precaution to guard against hidden weapons, even hand grenades.

The Japanese fought hard for the Marshalls. A Japanese soldier lies where he fell as two Marines inch up the beach of Parry Island, Eniwetok Atoll.

Infantrymen of the Fifth Army advance over the rugged Italian terrain; a German casualty lies in their path to Rome.

Marine dead, Eniwetok, Marshall Islands, D-Day, 1944.

Building the Atlantic Wall: conscript laborers from conquered countries working on German defenses along the coast of France to meet the inevitable Allied invasion.

Typical gun emplacement, Atlantic Wall (the photo was taken after the invasion, during which the position was bombarded from the sea).

An American reconnaissance photo of a portion of the Normandy coast showing some of Rommel's antilanding obstacles in place at low tide, May 1944.

The night jump of paratroopers had its hazards. Winds often blew the men away from landing area; some landed in swamps and streams and drowned and others were caught in trees where they could be shot by the enemy.

Bloody Omaha Beach, where the American infantrymen were pinned down by stubborn German opposition; for several hours it appeared that the men on Omaha had been stopped.

After heavy fighting, considerable improvisation, and imaginative leadership, troops begin moving inland from Omaha Beach.

The Canadian 3rd Division on Juno Beach encountered stiff resistance, but, once clear of the beach, moved to the Caen-Bayeux highway.

A British naval command post on the Normandy beachhead.

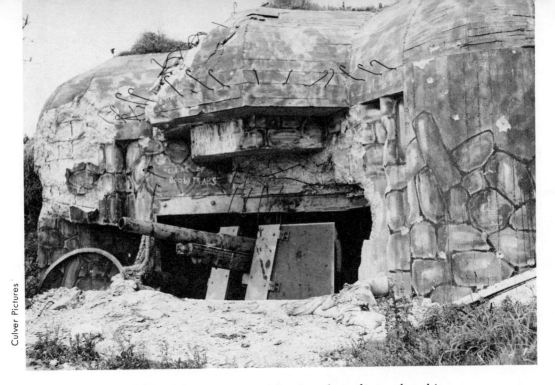

A battered German gun position; just above the gun barrel is a chalked inscription, "Clear of Booby Traps." German booby traps were left for unwary or souvenir-hunting GIs.

King George VI visits Normandy shortly after the invasion; behind him: hero of El Alamein, commander of the Twenty-first Army Group, Field Marshal Bernard Law Montgomery.

30033 A.C.

Vengeance weapons: shortly after the Normandy landings, German flying bombs and rockets began falling on Britain. A V-1 "buzz bomb" is about to fall into Piccadilly, London. The V-2, a more powerful rocket, rises out of its site in France and heads for somewhere in England. Londoners sift the wreckage of a shop in Smithfield Market hit by a V-2 rocket. More than a hundred were killed and 123 seriously injured by this one rocket. A buzz bomb is met by a hail of flak as it passes through a nighttime sky. Flak guns were frequently successful in knocking down buzz bombs.

The Allied advance, after breaking out of the Normandy beachheads, was held up by stiffened German resistance and the rugged French hedgerow country. By July 18, after suffering heavy casualties, the Allies took St. Lô.

A German officer surrenders to an American GI, France.

The invasion of Southern France, August 15; American and British paratroopers drift to earth behind the invasion beaches.

*While the invasion of
Southern France was
remarkably successful, it
was not uncontested by
the German defenders.
An American lies on the
invasion beach.*

An American Coast Guard gun crew in action, Southern France.

General de Gaulle arrives in France, June 14, 1944; he is here in discussion with French and British officers on the Normandy beachhead. On August 15 he would march triumphantly into Paris.

The Red Cross arrives in Southern France to bring the amenities to the battle zone. The second lady ashore is sporting the very popular saddle shoes of the period.

The National Archives

French tribute to a liberator: a homemade cross marks the grave of a dead GI. Inscription on the scrap of paper reads, "Died for France."

Imperial War Museum, London

No roof: incendiary bombs rain from the bomb bay of a British Lancaster. The target is Duisburg, the industrial center of the Ruhr.

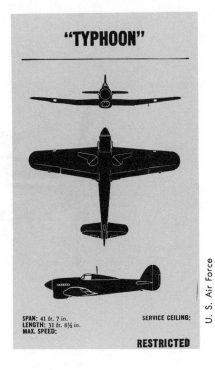

"TYPHOON"

SPAN: 41 ft. 7 in.
LENGTH: 31 ft. 8½ in.
MAX. SPEED:

SERVICE CEILING:

RESTRICTED

The business end of a Hawker Typhoon. Heavily armed, this fighter-bomber served in several capacities, from bombing to train-busting. With its four 20-mm. cannons, the Typhoon could destroy a locomotive.

American industrial capability was an important factor in the outcome of the war—mass production of tools, vehicles, weapons, and other war supplies helped to overwhelm the Axis. Photo shows but one aircraft factory turning out Liberator bombers. These planes were used by the U. S. Army, the Navy, and some Allied air forces.

North American P-51 Mustang, claimed by many to be the best fighter of the war. Originally designed for the British, the P-51 was adapted by the U. S. Army Air Forces. Equipped with a drop fuel tank, the Mustang could escort bombers to and from practically any target in Germany.

The Republic P-47 Thunderbolt, a powerful, tough aircraft; it too was capable of long-distance escort flights. The long-range fighter plane turned the tide of battle in the air. The P-47s, like the P-51s, were also widely used in the Pacific.

Lockheed P-38 Lightning, designed as a high-altitude interceptor, was the only American twin-engined fighter. Its speed and rugged construction made it especially effective against the Japanese Zero. In Europe it served as a fighter as well as a reconnaissance aircraft.

The backbone of the Luftwaffe's fighter squadrons from the beginning of the war was the Messerschmitt Me-109, this one being a "G," the last of the line. The Me-109 was flown on all European fronts, from North Africa to Russia. By 1944 it was inferior to Allied fighter aircraft.

Focke-Wulf FW-190 became operational after the outbreak of the war. For a time it could outfight the Spitfire, but later, more advanced models of the British fighter held their own. In the air battle of Germany, the FW-190 was a tough contender; some were armed with rockets that were fired into Allied bomber formations.

The Messerschmitt Me-262, the first jet fighter to be widely used in combat (the British were actually first with such a plane but did not use it). Luckily for the Allies, Hitler interfered with the production and utilization of the Me-262, which was not used against the bombers until late in the war. No Allied fighter could match its speed of more than 500 mph.

Fifth Air Force B-25s seeding a Japanese air base near Wewak, New Guinea, with "parafrag" bombs. Parachutes made the precise, low-level delivery possible; the B-25s could fly out of range before the bombs detonated.

Invasion force bound for Sansapor, on the westernmost point of northern New Guinea. Japanese troops in New Guinea were isolated and MacArthur turned his attention northward, to the Philippines.

Admiral William Halsey, exponent of naval air power, Secretary of the Navy Frank Knox, and Admiral Chester Nimitz, Commander in Chief, Pacific Fleet.

The National Archives

A wounded Marine is given first aid by buddies inland from the beaches. They were met with small-arms, mortar, and some artillery fire.

One of the major objectives of the Saipan invasion was Aslito Field—an air base less than 1,500 miles from Tokyo. Marines view the result of a Japanese attempt to retake the field in an early morning attack.

U. S. Air Force

Kamikaze attempt; a Japanese torpedo bomber, hit by antiaircraft batteries, attempts to crash into the deck of the escort carrier Sangamon. The plane fell into the sea.

MacArthur's return to the Philippines (to his right: Filipino President Sergio Osmeña). Splashing ashore, MacArthur said, "People of the Philippines, I have returned." This was a promise kept after three long years.

*Battle for Leyte Gulf: the Japanese carrier Zuiho, camou-
flaged to appear like a battleship from above, under attack
by planes from the* Enterprise. *The Japanese lost all four of
their carriers in the battle.*

*Chinese civilian laborers constructing an air base. Rocks were
hauled and broken up by hand. When completed, this will be a
base for the B-29 Superfortress; a Douglas C-47 transport flies
overhead.*

The year 1944 saw a definite turn of tide in favor of the Allies in the CBI. With sufficient supplies and men, they began regaining areas of Burma that had long been under Japanese domination. British troops on the move receive supplies by air in Burma.

A great Allied push in the Myitkyina sector, northern Burma, helped to clear the Myitkyna–Mandalay railroad into China. The Royal Scotch Fusiliers (British 36th Division) ford a jungle stream to musical accompaniment.

American prisoners in the wake of the
Waffen SS: Kampfgruppe Peiper. Rather
than be burdened by prisoners Peiper
merely slaughtered them; at Five
Corners, southwest of Malmédy,
Belgium, these GIs (a total of 86) were
shot by Peiper in what became known
as the "Malmédy Massacre."

Wary GIs in St. Vith;
though encircled and two
thirds captured, the
inexperienced 106th Division,
with its cooks and bakers
armed, held out until
reinforcements arrived. But
St. Vith was abandoned on
December 21.

The thrust of the German
counterattack in the Bulge
was subject to the weather
conditions. Begun in poor
weather, it succeeded, but
when the weather cleared—
beginning December 23—
Allied fighters and fighter-
bombers swooped down upon
German armored columns.
Ninth Air Force planes
have just destroyed an
American Sherman tank and
a half-track that had been
captured by the Germans.

1945

Watch this Victory...

EARLY in the morning of January 1, 1945, the Luftwaffe, in a surprising revivification, suddenly swooped from out of the morning mists and attacked several Allied airfields in France, Belgium, and Holland. More than 800 German planes participated in what Goering would call *Der Grosse Schlag* (The Great Blow). It was the Luftwaffe's contribution to Hitler's "Watch on the Rhine." Goering promised Hitler 3,000 planes but managed to scrape up only 900. To fly the planes, Goering had to employ irreplaceable experienced pilots and vulnerable student pilots.

Most of the Allied planes were caught on the ground, but retaliation came swiftly. The Luftwaffe struck at 17 fields and succeeded in destroying 156 aircraft (120 British, 36 American) in exchange for more than 200 Messerschmitts and Focke-Wulfs—and their pilots. Only 60 German pilots were taken prisoner; the rest, including a number of the Luftwaffe's best air leaders, had been thrown away in a grandstand gesture.

Even as the German fighters strafed and were shot down over the Allied fields in the north, Hitler launched "Operation Northwind" in the south. Assuming that Eisenhower had rushed all possible troops to the Ardennes, Hitler struck in Alsace, aiming a double-pronged blow against the American Seventh Army toward the city of Strasbourg. This attempt failed also, but it took nearly all of January to stop the Germans.

By the end of January the Allies had flattened the Bulge in the Ardennes and were preparing for the drive into the Rhineland. Hitler's last offensives had been costly to the Allies, but even more wasteful for the Germans: more than 125,000 casualties, including the reserves that might have served in the coming battle of Germany. Also lost were hundreds of planes and tanks.

A B-24, its left inboard engine smoking, flies through flak-filled skies over Germany. Although the Luftwaffe had been crippled by fuel shortages and a lack of experienced pilots, flak continued to take its toll of the Allied planes bombing Germany.

By early 1945, with Allies in command of the air, Berlin itself received nearly daily visits from the Eighth Air Force and RAF Bomber Command, based in Britain, and the Fifteenth Air Force in Italy. By war's end Berlin had become the most bombed city in Germany, with 6,340 acres of its main area destroyed and an estimated 50,000 Berliners killed by air raids alone.

By 1945 the Allied heavy bombers were able to roam the German skies with near impunity. General Doolittle had made a controversial, and much criticized, decision. Instead of being tied to the bombers as had been the necessary practice in the past, the Mustangs, Thunderbolts, and Lightnings were permitted to range afield and attack German aircraft wherever found, in the air and on the ground.

Refugees, particularly those fleeing from the Russians in the east, began pouring into the city of Dresden, greatly swelling the population, civil and military. Though known best for its many architectural treasures, Dresden also produced machine tools, optical instruments, and chemicals (which gave rise to the rumor that poison gas was manufactured there). It was also a rail hub. The Russians requested that the Allies bomb the rail facilities to interfere with troop movements to both fronts—and with the evacuation of refugees. After the war the Allies

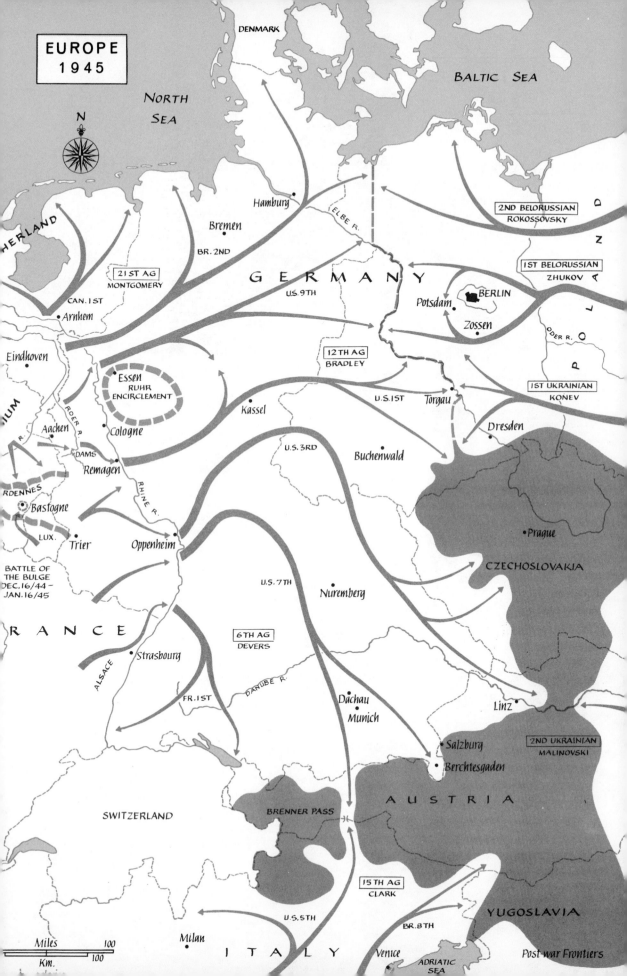

EUROPE
1945

N

NORTH
SEA

DENMARK

BALTIC SEA

HERLAND

Hamburg

Bremen

BR. 2ND

GERMANY

ELBE R.

2ND BELORUSSIAN
ROKOSSOVSKY

21ST AG
MONTGOMERY

CAN. 1ST

US. 9TH

Potsdam

BERLIN

1ST BELORUSSIAN
ZHUKOV

Arnhem

Zossen

ODER R.

POLAND

Eindhoven

12TH AG
BRADLEY

Essen
RUHR
ENCIRCLEMENT

Kassel

U.S.1ST

Torgau

1ST UKRAINIAN
KONEV

BIUM

Aachen

ROER R.

Cologne

Dresden

DAMS

R.

Remagen

RHINE R.

U.S. 3RD

Buchenwald

RDENNES

Bastogne

LUX.

Trier

Oppenheim

Prague

CZECHOSLOVAKIA

BATTLE OF
THE BULGE
DEC.16/44 –
JAN.16/45

RANCE

Strasbourg

U.S. 7TH

Nuremberg

6TH AG
DEVERS

ALSACE

FR.1ST

DANUBE R.

Dachau

Munich

Linz

2ND UKRAINIAN
MALINOVSKI

Salzburg

Berchtesgaden

SWITZERLAND

BRENNER PASS

AUSTRIA

15TH AG
CLARK

YUGOSLAVIA

Miles   100

U.S.5TH

BR.8TH

Post-war Frontiers

Km.   100

Milan

ITALY

Venice

ADRIATIC
SEA

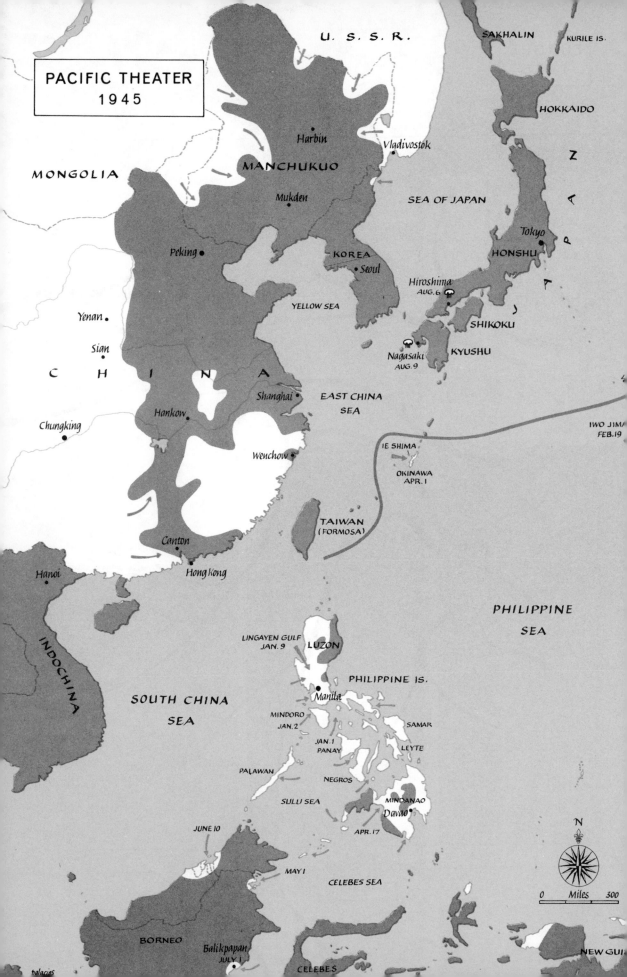

were accused of merely demonstrating to the Germans as well as the Russians just what they could do with their air might, that what occurred at Dresden on February 13–14, 1945, was a deliberate terror bombing of little military value.

Dresden had escaped bombing throughout most of the war excepting for an attack on its marshaling yards in October 1944 and again in January 1945 and was considered one of Germany's safest cities. The turn of military events apparently made it important in February. Bomber Command's Lancasters came over during the night of February 13 leaving behind a furiously burning city; the more than 800 bombers were hardly diverted by ineffectual flak batteries around Dresden or the all but nonexistent German night fighters. The next day 300 American Flying Fortresses came in to pour more explosives into the flame and smoke. The combination of high explosives, incendiaries, and weather conditions produced a frightful fire storm even more severe than that at Hamburg and destroyed about three quarters of Dresden, 1,600 square acres of ruin. The estimates of the dead range from a conservative 35,000 to the more probable 135,000. The bombing of Dresden was the most catastrophic single aerial attack of the war—and the last large-scale bombing of any German city.

The ruins of Dresden (after Russian occupation); though somewhat cleared, the intensity of the damage by air bombardment is evident.

Sovfoto

Infantrymen of the American 90th Division pass through the breached Siegfried Line at Habscheid, Germany.

The Fourth Front—the air—had diminished by 1945 with so many of Germany's industrial cities in virtual ruin. Even Hitler's last miracle weapon, the jet-propelled Messerschmitt 262, was used against the bombers too late to be effective. Hitler had chosen to waste that formidable defensive weapon in vengeance attacks, hoping to use the plane as a bomber. The function of the Me-262 was perverted and then, when it was finally used against the American bomber streams, the fuel shortage curtailed its missions.

There was movement on the remaining fronts on the churned-up ground. On January 12 three Russian armies began pushing through Poland, reaching the Oder River in the north and the Neisse in the south by mid-April. The Russians by-passed the heavily fortified city of Poznan and flowed toward Germany; one army, the First Belorussian Front, moved into a broad line on the Oder on February 3, just 36 miles east of Berlin.

At the southern end of the Eastern Front the Russian armies moved northwestward through the Danube Valley and into Budapest, despite heavy German fighting and counterattacks, on February 13. Determined to regain the Danube River line, Hitler ordered the Sixth Panzer Army transferred from the Ardennes, on the Western Front, to Hungary, where it accomplished nothing. Overwhelmed by the Second and Third

*American fighter-bombers strike a railyard at Torgen, Germany, at
the same time setting an adjacent oil refinery afire, denying the
German defenders both transportation and fuel.*

Ukrainian Armies, the Germans fell back; on March 30 the Russians
crossed into Austria. Vienna fell on April 13.

From yet another direction, in Italy, the Allies under General Clark,
after breaking into the Po Valley, drove the Germans before them toward Austria. The flight by the Germans from Italy, harried by Allied
aircraft, became a rout. Equipment and vehicles were abandoned and
hundreds of thousands of prisoners were taken; by the end of April the
fighting in Italy was over.

After regrouping on the Oder-Neisse line the Russians resumed their
drive toward Berlin on April 16; by the twenty-first, Russian troops had
reached the outskirts of the German capital. Three days later Berlin,
harboring a deluded, suicidal Hitler, was encircled.

In the west the Allies began their drive to the Rhine on February 8.
Eisenhower assigned the main push to Montgomery's Twenty-first Army
Group in the north, spearheaded by the Canadian First Army. To the
south, Bradley's Twelfth Army Group, in a somewhat subsidiary role (at
Montgomery's insistence), would send its First Army to capture the
Roer dams beyond Aachen. The Germans destroyed one of the dams,
flooding the river and delaying the campaign. The Canadians also ran
into a powerful German Army Group H, under General Student, which

261

An American soldier studies the still-standing bridge at Remagen, over which the Allies streamed across the Rhine into central Germany.

led to slow-moving, casualty-choked fighting. Terrain and weather too contributed to the misery and minor advances.

On February 23, Lieutenant Courtney H. Hodges' First Army crossed the swollen Roer, moved northward to assist the American Ninth Army, heading toward Cologne; other units of the First Army swerved southward. By March 5 the Allies had captured Cologne on the Rhine. Farther south Patton penetrated the Siegfried Line and pushed past Trier some 15 miles inside Germany.

Despite his field commanders' outcries, Hitler insisted that the German line be held on the west bank of the Rhine (a strategic withdrawal to the east bank would have provided a better defensive position; crossing the river under fire would have been costly for the Allies). The German defenses suffered from confusion, contradictory orders, and desperation. This undoubtedly explained why, when the First Army's 9th Armored Division approached the Rhine at Remagen in the afternoon of March 7, it found the Ludendorff railroad bridge still standing.

The Remagen Bridge (as it was more popularly known) was rushed by a rifle platoon while the Germans attempted to set off the charges

The Big Three, Churchill, Roosevelt and Stalin with military advisers at Livadia Palace in Yalta, February 9, 1945.

that were to have demolished the bridge. Little damage was done and American troops crossed the Rhine into Germany. Although Remagen had not been selected as one of the Rhine bridgeheads, Eisenhower seized the opportunity and poured reinforcements and supplies over it. Despite German attempts to retake the bridge, artillery fire and bombings by the Luftwaffe, the Remagen Bridge stood for ten days before collapsing into the river. In the meantime, engineers had built alternate spans across the Rhine.

Hitler blamed Rundstedt for the loss of the bridge, dismissed him, and put Field Marshal Albert Kesselring in command of the Western Front. There was little that Kesselring could have accomplished on his crumbling Italian front; he arrived in Germany only to be handed another doomed front.

Marshal Georgi K. Zhukov,
who saved Leningrad,
Moscow, and Stalingrad,
led the Red Army into Berlin.

Torgau, on the Elbe River, Germany. A Russian soldier
greets an American GI on April 25, 1945.

Patton, meanwhile, had continued his race for the Rhine and discovered a bridgehead at Oppenheim; before dawn of March 23, six of his infantry battalions had crossed the river. Montgomery, although with less dash, fought a carefully planned campaign using heavy air attacks, great artillery barrages, and airborne drops, also crossed the Rhine on March 23. The Allies could now encircle the Ruhr, isolating it to avoid costly fighting, and continue a broad sweep through Germany.

It had been agreed that the Russians would take Berlin and that the Allies would move into Germany roughly to the Elbe River, on a line about 60 miles west of the German capital. Many were unhappy about this agreement, insisting that the Allies were turning over great pieces of Europe to the Soviets. Patton, for one, was dejected and would have been delighted to continue through Berlin on to Moscow. Montgomery also suggested the drive to Berlin.

Eisenhower's cooler head prevailed and, conceding that wars are "waged in pursuance of political aims," regarded an Allied drive to Berlin as "militarily unsound."

Following the encirclement of the Ruhr, the Allied advance to the Elbe proceeded at a remarkable rate as the German defenses disintegrated. The great Russian juggernaut was not to be stopped as hordes of well-equipped Soviets engulfed the defenders. From the time they had invaded Germany Russian soldiers were greeted with posters: *Red Army Soldier: You are now on German soil; the hour of revenge has struck!*

With this license, Russian troops left a wide swath of burned homes, looting, out and out robbery, and rape behind them. While it was worse in Germany, even those countries "liberated" by the Russians, Poland and the Baltic states suffered as much at the hands of their liberators as their captors. Stories of Russian Army atrocities began circulating and eventually a curb was placed—read "executions"—on the offenders.

On April 20, Hitler celebrated his fifty-sixth birthday deep underground in Berlin; he even ventured with a few friends into the gardens of his Reich Chancellery, from which he could hear the boom of the Russian guns. On the same day the American Seventh Army took Nuremberg. Two days later Hitler announced that he would remain in Berlin to direct the final battle against Germany's "deadly enemies the Jewish Bolsheviks." On April 23, Churchill and the new American President Harry Truman rejected an offer of surrender from Gestapo chief Heinrich Himmler, whom Hitler had appointed Commander in Chief of the Home Army. Enraged, Hitler fired Himmler, who saw no further reason to remain in a doomed Berlin and he headed for the Allied lines. On the same day Hitler also fired Goering, preparing to flee from his secluded country home Karinhall, after the Luftwaffe chief offered to take over for Hitler, trapped in Berlin. It was not a good day for Hitler, for the Russians had also broken into central Berlin.

On April 25 a patrol of the American First Army made contact with Russian troops on the Elbe at Torgau. Units of the Allied Sixth Army Group, under the command of General Jacob L. Devers, pushed southward toward Austria and linked with Clark's 15th Army Group in the area of Brenner Pass. Germany was literally cut to pieces.

In the ruins of his Third Reich, which he had promised would survive for a thousand years, Hitler acted out the final mad act of the drama. He married his mistress of many years, Eva Braun, and he appointed Admiral Karl Doenitz as Supreme Commander of the Wehrmacht and Reich President; the hapless Doenitz had neither an army nor a country. As Russian shells began falling into the Reich Chancellery gardens, Hitler learned of the assassination of Mussolini and his mistress, captured while attempting to slip into Switzerland. On April 30, Eva Braun Hitler took poison and Hitler shot himself after giving orders that their bodies were to be cremated in the garden.

With their former, no-surrender Supreme Commander gone, the German forces were free to give up the hopeless battle with impunity. The surrender in Italy occurred on the day of Hitler's wedding, April 29; on the day of his suicide, the Russians had reached the Reichstag building. Near Munich members of the American Seventh Army overran another concentration camp, Dachau, and found it difficult to believe what they saw.

German armies on the Eastern Front fled to the west seeking Allied sanctuary; three army remnants were permitted to pass through the American lines before the gap was closed; another three were taken by the Russians—about 2,000,000 men became prisoners of war for years. The capitulations followed: on May 4 German forces in Holland, Denmark, and northwest Germany surrendered to Montgomery; in the south they surrendered to Devers' American Sixth Army Group on May 5.

Following negotiations, Eisenhower refused to accept a unilateral agreement insisting that the Russians participate and that the surrender be "unconditional." The German representatives, led by General Alfred Jodl, were dismayed, but after consultation with Doenitz, and with a Russian representative present, signed the surrender at Eisenhower's headquarters at Rheims.

Jodl wept on May 7, 1945, as he signed the papers. Throughout Europe and the United States the next day, V-E Day (Victory in Europe), there were also tears, but of joy as Europe's most devastating, most wasteful war ended. On May 9 the surrender was officially ratified in Berlin, where Field Marshal Keitel appeared at Marshal Georgi Zhukov's headquarters to sign for Germany.

Victory did not bring instant peace. But it did stop the killing and, after nearly six years of slaughter and destruction, V-E Day seemed to

Grand Admiral Karl Doenitz, who commanded the German submarine fleet throughout World War II; in 1943 he became the Commander in Chief of the German Navy. At war's end Hitler designated Doenitz as his successor as commander of Germany's armed forces and head of the German state. Doenitz hoped to manipulate the British and Americans into a separate peace and to continue the war in the East, but the Allies demanded, and got, an unconditional surrender on both fronts.

Field Marshal Keitel signing a second surrender document at Zhukov's headquarters near Berlin on May 9, 1945. Russian histories tend to ignore the earlier surrender at Rheims.

American landings on Luzon were not strongly opposed, but the fight for Manila was bloody, after which the Japanese dug into several pockets in the mountains north and east of Manila. These positions were murderous to approach and take out. One method to clear the pockets of resistance was to drop belly tanks filled with napalm into caves and foxholes.

bring the dawn of a brighter new day, at last, to a long-suffering humanity.

Sergeant Marc Blitzstein, serving with the Eighth Air Force in Britain, composed a work for chorus, orchestra, and soloists entitled *The Airborne.*

Inspired by the fall of Mussolini and the surrender of Italy, Blitzstein, with characteristic humanism, observed:

> *Thankfulness, not without grief.*
> *The bright morning, not without warning.*
> *Watch this victory:*
> *Whose victory? Whose glory*
>
> *Watch this victory.*

The bombings of Germany long after Marc Blitzstein wrote those lines proved him to be a prophet. Air power, unleashed, literally eliminated several German cities from the map.

An even more stunning use of the air weapon would be demonstrated in the Pacific.

Japanese fire from the front and the flank (Mount Suribachi) scattered Marine wreckage on the beach—this was the Japanese plan that nearly worked. But the Marines persevered. Reinforcements and supplies came in under artillery, rocket, mortar, and small-arms fire.

Marines on the sifting volcanic ash of Red Beach, Iwo Jima. The coarse ash clogged weapons, caused temporary blindness when a near miss scattered it, and got into wounds, which complicated treatment. Men of the 4th Marine Division are pinned down on the shore.

By the first of the year the Leyte campaign, except for small mopping-up operations of isolated pockets of Japanese, was over. The next step: taking Luzon, the largest of the Philippine Islands. While Australian troops attended to Japanese still in New Guinea, New Britain, and other isolated points, including Borneo, the American Eighth Army cleared and occupied the smaller islands south of Luzon, Samar and Mindoro. Then on January 9, 1945, General Walter Krueger's Sixth Army began landing operations at Lingayen Gulf. They were expected and permitted to land without serious opposition—although the prelanding phase was made a nightmare for the assisting Seventh Fleet by swarms of kamikaze aircraft that sank no less than 17 ships and damaged 50 more.

General Tomoyuki Yamashita had no illusions about holding Luzon, but his Fourteenth Area Army offered the Americans a stiff and bitter resistance. The outskirts of Manila were reached on February 3, but the Japanese held out for a month before slipping northward into the mountains, forming eventually into three pockets. By August 14, except for such pockets, which faced greater danger from starvation than from American guns, all serious Japanese resistance on Luzon was over. Of the original 250,000 men of the Fourteenth Area Army, about 170,000 died; the American losses numbered 8,000 dead and 30,000 wounded.

The plan for the Central Pacific was to complete the occupation of the Philippines and then move in closer to the Japanese home islands by an invasion of Okinawa, which was just 350 miles south of Kyushu, the southernmost large island of Japan. Okinawa could serve as a base for aerial operations as well as the projected invasions of Japan itself. As an aid in the B-29 air campaign against Japan, it was decided to take a roughly eight-square-mile island in the Volcano Islands. This was Iwo Jima, situated between Japan and the B-29 bases in the Marianas.

The Japanese again expected the Americans and prepared for their coming by creating a defensive system, interconnected by underground labyrinths (often as deep as 35 feet), capable of withstanding heavy bombardment from ship or plane. Lieutenant General Tadamichi Kuribayashi, the architect of forbidding anthills, commanded about 23,000 crack troops.

The assault began, following three days of heavy bombardment, on the morning of February 19, when troops of the Marine 4th and 5th Divisions were set ashore and moved inland about 300 yards, cutting across Iwo Jima's narrow neck at the southern end of the island. To the Marines' left rose the island's most prominent feature, 550-foot-high Mount Suribachi. To their right lay two completed airfields and another under construction. These were the prizes on this tiny, otherwise worthless, island of volcanic rock and ash. For the Marines, the battle for Iwo Jima would prove to be the toughest in the Corps' 169-year history.

Having established their beachhead, the Marines wondered at light re-

Japanese snipers used Okinawan huts for cover and were extinguished by flame-throwers, weapons that were widely used on Okinawa against dug-in Japanese. These GIs move toward Kadena Airfield.

sistance during the 4,000-yard rush to the beach and the landing operations. The lull lasted for about 20 minutes, and then from various positions the Japanese artillery and mortars opened up. The 5th Marines fought for three days to secure Mount Suribachi, bristling with gun emplacements and honeycombed with burrows and caves, each of which had to be taken out individually.

After Suribachi, the bulk of Iwo Jima remained to be taken. The fighting was brutal, hand to hand, with bayonet, flame-thrower, grenade, and rifle. The Japanese soldiers, sworn to kill ten Americans before dying themselves, were waiting in a webwork of pillboxes and bunkers connected by caves.

The fighting continued for 26 days before, on March 16, the island was declared secure. Twelve days before that the first B-29, damaged in a raid on Japan, fluttered into Iwo Jima—the first example of Iwo's value and justification for the dreadful battle.

Although Iwo Jima was pronounced "secure," the final banzai charge was staged by 300 Japanese soldiers ten days later; it accomplished nothing. The final grim, fruitless battle ended with practically all of the Japanese dead along with a number of Marines. The estimated number

The incursions of the Superfortresses were met by Japanese fighters such as the Kawasaki Hien (Flying Swallow but named "Tony" by American Intelligence). First introduced in combat over New Guinea in 1943, the Tony suffered from engine defects but was widely used in home defense. Tony pilots frequently rammed the B-29s in a tai atari (suicide crash).

of Japanese killed in the taking of Iwo Jima was 21,000; over 5,000 Marines gave their lives for an unlovely, static aircraft carrier. By early April it was possible for P-51 fighters based on Iwo Jima to join up with B-29s from the Marianas and escort them to the Japanese home islands and back.

The next step in the Central Pacific was to move to Okinawa, in the Ryukyu Islands. With its fine airfields, anchorages, and proximity to the islands of Japan, Okinawa could serve as the perfect base for the planned invasions of Japan. Originally scheduled for March 1, the Okinawa landings were delayed a month by the exigencies of Luzon and Iwo Jima. As at the other islands, the Japanese anticipated the American operations and meticulously prepared their defenses. As at Iwo, they went underground and planned to make the battle as costly as possible to the Americans. The slogan of the Japanese 32nd Army, defending Okinawa, was "One plane for one warship. One boat for one ship. One man for ten enemy. One man for one tank." The final objective was not victory, but to bleed the Allied forces to death and ultimate discouraging defeat.

"At 0830 in the morning of 1 April 1945," wrote Major General Lemuel C. Shepherd, Jr., commander of the 6th Marines during the invasion, "on Easter Sunday, assault elements of the United States Tenth Army, comprising the Third Marine Amphibious Corps, XXIV Corps, Tactical Air Force, and other units, commenced landing on the western beaches of Okinawa to begin the final great amphibious operation of

272

*Superfortresses practically unchallenged, fly past snow-capped
Mount Fuji, central Honshu—Tokyo is a mere sixty miles distant.*

World War II, an 82-day campaign that was marked by some of the bitterest fighting in the Pacific War."

Lieutenant General Mitsuru Ushijima's plan was to permit the landings and then deal with the invaders in an attritional drawn-out defense. By evening some 50,000 American troops had come ashore near the southern end of the narrow 75-mile-long island, forming a beachhead about six miles long and three deep. The 6th Marines quickly seized Yonton Airfield to the north, and the Army's 7th and 96th Divisions, turning to the south, took Kadena Airfield. Landing with the Marines, correspondent Ernie Pyle noted that "We had landed absolutely unopposed, which is indeed an odd experience for a Marine. We didn't expect it to continue—a Marine doesn't fool himself like that."

The Marine Corps turned to the north and cleared out about three quarters of the island, encountering tough resistance on Motobu Peninsula and tiny Ie Shima, just off the peninsula (where Pyle was killed by a sniper) by April 16. The northern portion of Okinawa was secured by April 19. In its southern push, it was the Army that first battered against

273

Crew of the Enola Gay, *Tinian, Mariana Islands, August 1945:* (front)
*Staff Sergeant George R. Caron; Sergeant Joe S. Stiborik; Sergeant Wyatt
E. Duzenbury; Private First Class Richard H. Nelson; Sergeant Robert
H. Shumard;* (back row) *Major Robert Thomas Ferebee; Captain Theo-
dore J. Van Kirk; Colonel Paul W. Tibbets, Jr.; and Captain Robert A.
Lewis. The plane was named for pilot Tibbets' mother.*

the formidable Japanese defense system, a series of fortifications dug
into the ridges of the hilly terrain across the narrow island.

It took from April 6 to April 24 for the Tenth Army (Marines and
U. S. Army) to break through the Machinato Line and from April 28 to
May 31 to breach the Shuri Line, only to run into yet another defensive
line cutting the island from east to west near the southern tip. Even then
the savage battling continued until June 21, except for spotty disorganized resistance. During the final phase of the Okinawa campaign,
Lieutenant General Simon Bolivar Buckner, Tenth Army commander,
became one of the numerous casualties when he was killed in the front
lines by a Japanese artillery shell.

Other casualties of the Okinawa campaign were the island's commander, Lieutenant General Ushijima, and his Chief of Staff, Major
General Isamu Cho, who committed *hara-kiri* with a ceremonial knife
and a sword. The last sounds they heard on June 22 were those of
American hand grenades bursting near their cave.

274

A mushroom cloud forcefully rises above the clouds; the birth of the Atomic Age, August 6, 1945.

For the first time in their Pacific fighting the Marines had encountered a civilian population. The Japanese had indoctrinated the Okinawans with the belief that in order to become a Marine a man first had to kill his parents. Rather than face captivity—and worse—by the Americans, Okinawans committed suicide. Many leaped from cliffs onto rock-strewn beaches, throwing their young children before them. Husbands slaughtered their wives and then held hand grenades to their own throats.

Military dead, among the Japanese, amounted to over 100,000 (with a possible 20,000 entombed in caves); about 7,000 prisoners, Japanese and Okinawan, were taken. American losses were 4,379 Army troops killed and 17,558 wounded; the Marines lost 3,440 dead and 15,487 wounded. The U. S. Navy, too, paid heavily for Okinawa, suffering 4,907 killed and 4,824 wounded. Indeed, a victory to be scrutinized.

The extremely high casualties among the Navy men were primarily inflicted by Japanese aircraft, most of them kamikaze attacks. Beginning in earnest on April 6, the Japanese, having recovered from the initial preinvasion air strikes on various airfields, unleashed the first of nearly 1,500 suicide-plane attacks. These succeeded in sinking over 30 American ships (destroyers, destroyer escorts, picket ships—none of battleship or carrier class) and damaging hundreds.

The great battleship *Yamato* was also assigned to make a "special attack." Spotted by American submarines on April 6, not long after leaving Tokuyama, the *Yamato* and company came under heavy attack from American carrier planes shortly after noon the following day. At the cost of 12 pilots (10 planes) the aircraft of Task Force 58 sent the world's largest superbattleship to the bottom of the East China Sea, along with four destroyers and a cruiser. Still some 270 miles from Okinawa, the *Yamato* sank without ever striking a decisive blow during the war. Its destruction marked the end of the age of the battleship.

The victory at Okinawa was cause for soul searching in the Allied High Command. The intensity of Japanese resistance did not make the projected invasions of the Japanese home islands—"Operation Olympic" in November 1945 and "Operation Coronet" in March 1946—very promising of anything but such killing as had been experienced at Iwo Jima and Okinawa. General MacArthur estimated that the invasions would result in about a million casualties.

Army commanders were certain that an invasion of Japan would be necessary before peace could come to the Pacific; U. S. Army Air Forces strategists disagreed, certain that the B-29 held the key to Japan's defeat. When the B-29s began operating out of China in June 1944, the missions were afflicted with mechanical as well as logistical problems. The Superfortress, rushed through its testing and production

Stark result of the atomic bomb blast, Hiroshima.

phases, revealed technical "bugs" during its early operations. Missions, in turn, could not be flown until supplies were flown into the Chinese bases. They were few and not successful.

When the Marianas were taken, the B-29s of 21st Bomber Command (under Brigadier General Haywood S. Hansell, Jr.) began flying to Japanese targets in November. The initial high-altitude missions proved disappointing and losses were high, several of the planes being lost in the Pacific. In January of 1945 Hansell was relieved by Major General Curtis E. LeMay, an experienced, tough combat veteran from the European Theater. LeMay, upon studying the problem (chiefly the high winds that blew at high altitudes over Japan), changed the tactic: the B-29s would bomb from low altitudes, which, he was certain, would improve accuracy. The objection was that low-altitude bombings would make it easier for Japanese fighters to attack the B-29s and, in addition, would expose them to antiaircraft fire. As it turned out, neither proved especially potent in stopping the B-29s. Also, the capture of Iwo Jima provided an easier-to-reach haven for the distressed B-29s.

277

Shigemitsu signs "By Command in behalf of the Emperor of Japan and the Japanese Government." Soon after MacArthur's voice boomed over the microphone: "These proceedings are closed!" The Second World War was over.

LeMay contributed one further element to his new technique: mass incendiary night bombings of Japanese industrial cities whose wooden structures were highly susceptible to fire. The first attack by more than 300 Superfortresses during the night of March 9/10 on Tokyo razed about a quarter of the city, killing more than 80,000, wounding 40,000, and leaving a million homeless. Militarily successful, the fire-bombing of Tokyo initiated a campaign against Japanese urban-industrial centers. Besides Tokyo, other major cities were desolated by fire: Nagoya, Kobe, Osaka, Yokohama, and Kawasaki. By mid-June, LeMay turned to the smaller cities, announcing his intentions to the civil—and military—population in advance, advising evacuation, by dropping warning leaflets. The fire raids were often followed by precision bombardments, to assure the destruction of less combustible factories.

Its industries in ruins, its population panicky and demoralized, its waters mined and controlled by the American Navy, Japan was defeated, but Japanese military leaders would not concede the unthinkable. When the Allies issued the Potsdam Declaration, demanding the unconditional surrender of Japan, late in July, it was immediately rejected, although the Emperor and the Cabinet expressed a willingness toward acceptance. The War Party in the government viewed the Declaration as a threat to the Emperor, the Japanese way of life—and, of course, to themselves. They also ignored a vague threat of "prompt and utter destruction" that came with the declaration—what could be worse than the fire raids?

The answer lay in the Marianas on Tinian, where a B-29 unit, the specially trained 509th Composite Group, had been stationed since early July. President Truman, en route to Washington in the mid-Atlantic, heard that Japanese Premier Kantaro Suzuki had rejected the surrender demand; Truman ordered the 509th to carry out the mission for which it was trained.

On August 6 the *Enola Gay,* a B-29 piloted by the group commander, Colonel Paul W. Tibbets, Jr., took off from Tinian—one aircraft carrying one bomb, accompanied by two other planes with observers. At 8:15 A.M. the *Enola Gay,* from an altitude of 31,600 feet, dropped its bomb. The explosion that followed rocked the B-29s racing from the scene, flooding their fuselages with bright light. One of the crew, observing the broiling cloud curling up from Hiroshima, could only gasp, "My God!"

Nearly five square miles of Hiroshima was converted into rubble and perhaps 80,000 people into nothingness. The *Enola Gay* had dropped the first atomic bomb. The wide-scale destruction and casualties were kept from the Japanese people, and the following day they were told that a so-called powerful new American bomb was no cause for alarm.

On August 8, Russia declared war on Japan and by the next day had begun invading southern Sakhalin, Manchuria, and northern Korea. Still the War Party in Japan held out, even attempting to interfere with the Emperor's plea for peace. His recorded appeal was eventually broadcast (although factions of the War Party—which was run by militarists Korechika Anami, Yoshijiro Umezu, and Soemu Toyoda—broke into the Imperial Palace in an attempt to destroy the recording).

But the broadcast came too late; a second atomic bomb was dropped on Nagasaki on August 9. Even so, as the Emperor advised for peace, War Minister Anami, Army Chief Umezu, and Navy Chief Toyoda pleaded for "one last battle" to be fought in Japan to preserve the nation's honor.

Hirohito persevered and demanded that Japan surrender the next day, but it was not until August 14, with the Tokyo War Council deadlocked, that Emperor Hirohito announced that Japan would surrender immediately. On August 15 his recording was broadcast, initiating a wave of national mourning and suicides and suicide attempts among the higher military leaders as well as some rebellion among the younger hotheads. There was even a plan to have kamikaze planes dive into the surrender ceremonies (fortunately these seven planes were lost somewhere between takeoff and their objective; their fate is still a mystery).

Hostilities in the Pacific ended on August 15, and the official surrender ceremonies took place aboard the battleship *Missouri*, anchored in Tokyo Bay, on September 2, 1945. General Douglas MacArthur later broadcast a message to the United States beginning with simple, moving statements: "Today the guns are silent. A great tragedy has ended. A great victory has been won . . .

"A new era is upon us," MacArthur continued. "Even the lesson of victory itself brings with it profound concern, both for our future security and the survival of civilization. The destructiveness of the war potential, through progressive advances in scientific discovery, has in fact now reached a point which revises the traditional concept of war . . ."

Watch this victory . . .

Two bazooka men of the 3rd Armored Division on the outlook for German panzers in the Ardennes; in mid-January 1945, when this photo was taken, the Germans were being pushed back out of the Bulge.

Artillery barrage opening the Roer River offensive, whose objective was Cologne, Germany.

Allied air forces held down the Luftwaffe and kept it from interfering with the Allied advances into Germany. Martin B-26 Marauders attack a German airfield.

While the British, French, and Americans moved in from the west, the Russians continued their rush from the east; in the vanguard, the power-ful T-34 tank. Its wide tracks made it a fine cross-country vehicle; its armor made it superior to most German tanks.

A once busy street corner in central Berlin; by early 1945 the Allied air forces were running out of strategic targets. Berlin remained Hitler's headquarters, however.

The ruins of Cologne, its buildings gutted by bombardment, its bridges down in the Rhine. Rail junction, river port, and metallurgy and chemical center, Cologne was the target of the first thousand-bomber raid.

Deep inside Germany, American troops fight across a small river; a German soldier lies at the river's edge.

Closing in from another direction; from the south, through Italy, French forces manning American tanks push through Austria.

Vice President Harry Truman and Roosevelt, who had been elected to an unprecedented fourth term in 1944; his sudden death in April 1945 placed Truman into the office of the President, where he would have to make one of the momentous decisions of the war: the use of a new weapon.

The death camps: as the Allies pierced deeper inside Germany, as well as occupied countries, they overran concentration camps where Hitler's enemies were slaughtered wholesale. An American tank crew is cheered by the freed inmates of a concentration camp at Lenz, Austria.

An American medical officer discovers a mass grave.

A German woman is sickened by the product of an extermination camp near Mannering, which she and others denied existed.

The Soviet flag is being placed above the ruins of the Reichstag, Berlin.

Sovfoto

Culver Pictures

The defeated: Field Marshal von Rundstedt, in full uniform and his face revealing the ravages of war, as a prisoner of war. With him is Lieutenant General Alexander M. Patch, commander of the American Seventh Division and director of the invasion of Southern France.

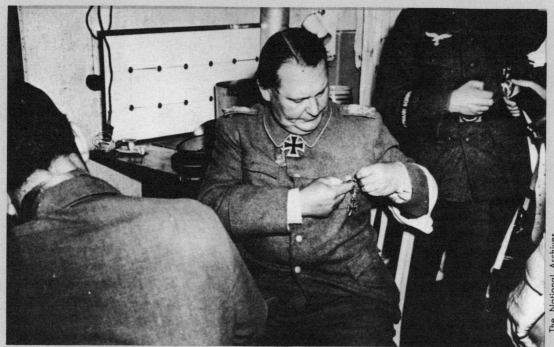

The National Archives

Hermann Goering, once second only to Hitler in the Reich, was stripped by Hitler at the end of all his Nazi Party positions. As a prisoner of war, he was also stripped of his decorations before being imprisoned. Condemned to death later at Nuremberg, Goering committed suicide.

Rheims, France, May 7, 1945, at Eisenhower's headquarters, where Field Marshal Jodl surrendered unconditionally. The Allies celebrate: Russian representative Major General Ivan Susloparoff; Lieutenant General Sir Frederick Morgan, Eisenhower's Deputy Chief of Staff; Lieutenant General Walter Bedell Smith, Chief of Staff; Captain Harry C. Butcher, naval aide to Eisenhower; Air Chief Marshal Sir Arthur Tedder, Deputy Supreme Commander; and Admiral Sir Harold M. Burrough, Allied naval chief.

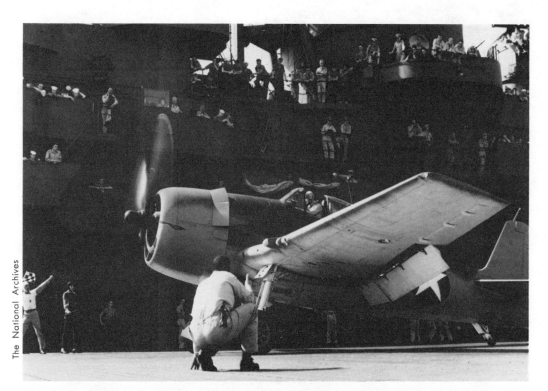

Carrier war: carrier-based aircraft played an important role in the final Pacific victory, but it was a part not without hazards. A Grumman Hellcat, a plane especially designed to deal with the Zero, prepares to take off from the new Yorktown *(replacement for the carrier lost at Midway); Hellcats proved themselves (and their pilots) in the Marianas Turkey Shoot and other Pacific battles.*

*Return to Corregidor.
Paratroopers have already
landed and amphibious troops
begin landing on the beach on
the tiny island where the last
American troops held out till
the end in 1942. Retaking
Corregidor required ten days
of hard fighting; in Luzon
proper, the hard-fighting
Japanese in the mountains held
out until the war ended.*

A hard landing and this Hellcat becomes a flaming wreck, killing its pilot.

Vought Corsairs, originally regarded as unusable aboard carriers (because of its high cockpit, its poor visibility, and a tendency for the plane to land with a bounce), were eventually accepted and proved effective. Widely used by the Marines, the Corsair was hated by the Japanese, who called it "Whistling Death," because of the sound it made in a dive. Radomes near right wing tips (housing radar equipment) indicate these planes were used in night missions.

A Hellcat's belly tank falls to the deck of the new Lexington (the old had been sunk in the Battle of the Coral Sea) and ignites. As the deck crew fights the flames, the pilot gets out of the cockpit.

Marine landing craft head for beaches at Iwo Jima, February 19, 1945, with Mount Suribachi (from which the Japanese had a perfect view of the landings); the Marines are about to begin one of their toughest battles.

Marine Curtiss Helldivers over Iwo Jima invasion beaches to assist in the assault—pinning down the Japanese during the critical landing phase.

*One of the most frightful weapons of the Pacific war was the
flame-thrower, the only weapon that could "neutralize" Japanese
dug into caves and tunnels. A Marine assault team moves in on
a Japanese position, Iwo Jima.*

*A Japanese flame-thrower casualty
(actually on Eniwetok; wherever
it occurred the horror
was the same).*

The first patrol reaches the top of Mount Suribachi, February 23. Men of the 28th Regiment, Fifth Marines, affix a flag to a piece of Japanese pipe—and keep a wary eye out for the enemy. Moments later a Japanese grenade landed nearby, damaging Sergeant Lou Lowery's camera but not the film.

The second flag raising, Iwo Jima. When the fighting on and around Mount Suribachi lessened later in the day, a second patrol was sent to the top to place a larger—more visible—flag on the summit. This is the classic photo by Joe Rosenthal. Of the six Marines who participated in the second flag raising, three left the island alive.

The Marine III Amphibious Corps, in amphtracks, ready for the run in on the beach at Okinawa, Easter Sunday, April 1, 1945. In the distance a battleship lays down a preparatory barrage.

A Marine Corsair unleashes a volley of 5-inch rockets against a Japanese stronghold in the hills of Okinawa.

For the first time in the Pacific war, the Marines encountered great numbers of civilians, the classic innocent victims of war. Those caught between the combatants fled the battlegrounds, taking their possessions with them.

Okinawa's proximity to the Japanese home islands intensified desperation of the defense, both on the island and at sea; kamikaze attacks became fierce and frequent. A Japanese dive bomber has smashed into the deck of the carrier Bunker Hill *off Okinawa, killing nearly 400 men, although the carrier did not sink.*

The National Archives

PRODUCTION CHART of GOODS and MANPOWER–WORLD WAR II

Tanks

	USA	Britain	Germany — Tanks, self-propelled guns, and assault-guns	Japan — Medium and light tanks	USSR
1940	300	1,400	1,600	Not available	2,800
1941	4,100	4,800	3,800	1,000	6,400
1942	25,000	8,600	6,300	1,200	24,700
1943	29,500	7,500	12,100	800	24,000
1944	17,600	4,600	19,000	300	29,000
1945	12,000	Not available	3,900 (Jan-Mar)	100 (Apr-July)	15,400 (Jan-June)

Warships

	USA	Britain — Displacement tons	Germany — Submarines only. Few major surface vessels were built during the war	Japan — Fiscal year	USSR
1940	52,600 (July-Dec)	263,200	23,800 tons	94,700	Not available
1941	219,300	437,200	147,800	225,200	
1942	859,500	481,400	193,000	254,000	
1943	2,667,400	609,600	211,400	230,100	
1944	3,176,800	583,400	275,300	468,400	
1945	1,190,000 (Jan-June)	312,800 (Jan-Sept)	54,900 (Jan-May)	66,700 (Apr-July)	

Merchant ships

	USA — Gross tons (ships of 2,000 tons and over)	Britain — Gross tons (ships of 100 tons and over)	Germany — Figures not available; production probably negligible	Japan — Gross tons (ships of 500 tons and over)	USSR
1940	444,700	810,000		293,600	Not available
1941	749,100	1,156,000		210,400	
1942	5,392,800	1,301,000		260,100	
1943	12,485,600	1,204,000		769,100	
1944	11,403,200	1,014,000		1,699,200	
1945	7,614,900	856,000 (Jan-Sept)		559,600 (Jan-Aug)	

Aircraft

	USA	Britain	Germany	Japan	USSR
1940	6,100	15,000	10,200	4,800	7,000
1941	19,400	20,100	11,000	5,100	12,500
1942	47,800	23,600	14,200	8,900	26,000
1943	85,900	26,200	25,200	16,700	37,000
1944	96,300	26,500	39,600	28,200	40,000
1945	46,000 (Jan-Aug)	12,100	Not available	11,100	35,000

Manpower

	USA — On June 30 of each year	Britain	Germany — On May 31 of each year	Japan	USSR
1940	458,300	2,212,000	5,600,000	1,723,200	2,500,000
1941	1,795,000	3,278,000	7,200,000	2,411,400	4,207,000
1942	3,844,500	3,784,000	8,600,000	2,829,400	9,000,000
1943	8,918,600	4,300,000	9,500,000	3,808,200	10,000,000
1944	11,241,200	4,500,000	9,100,000	5,365,000	12,400,000
1945	11,858,500	4,653,000	Not available	7,193,200 (Aug 1945)	10,800,000

Action in another area of the Pacific: Australian troops of I Corps landing at Balikpapan, Borneo (once the source of oil for the Japanese), in the last full-scale amphibious landing of the war, July 1, 1945.

A Japanese destroyer escort, its crew slipping into the China Sea, sinks after an attack by Air Apaches (the 345th Bomb Group); by the spring of 1945 the seas and the air surrounding Japan were controlled by the Allies.

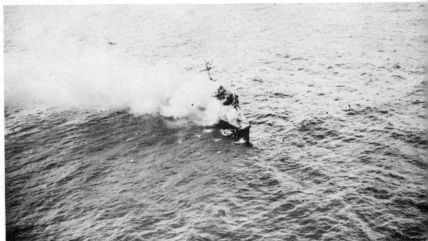

Operating out of airfields on Luzon, B-25s of the 345th Bomb Group attacked Japanese shipping along the China coast, cutting off supplies and reinforcements to Japanese troops isolated throughout the Pacific. A destroyer escort is under attack.

A Superfortress, escorted by P-51s picked up on the way to Tokyo (the fighters could not carry the heavy, elaborate navigational equipment). The B-29 would lead the way from and back to Iwo—and the Mustangs would protect the bombers all the way to the target and back.

Mitsubishi Raiden (Thunderbolt, code-named "Jack") was first encountered in the Marianas late in the war and was the most widely used interceptor during the B-29 missions against Japan.

Mission completed, the Enola Gay *returns to Tinian.*

Result of a B-29 fire raid: Toyama, an aluminum production center, burns after the night mission of August 1, 1945. All but .4 per cent of the city was destroyed.

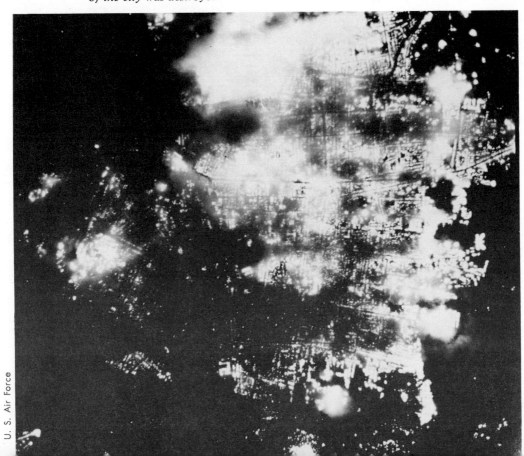

Tokyo after a fire bombing. More than 56 square miles of central Tokyo was burned out, destroying about 40 per cent of the Japanese capital.

The second bomb fell on Nagasaki on August 9, erasing an area 2.3 miles long and 1.9 miles wide. It was the final blow.

Desolation, Hiroshima; Japanese military men refused to accept the fact of defeat even in the light of Hiroshima.

Marines of the 5th Division begin the occupation of Japan at Yokosuka, a naval base. Building in the background is an aircraft factory.

General MacArthur, Supreme Commander for the Allied Powers in the Pacific (left), and Fleet Admiral Chester W. Nimitz arrive aboard the battleship Missouri in Tokyo Bay, September 2, 1945, for the surrender ceremonies.

The Japanese delegation on the deck of the Missouri; *top-hatted, formal, and grim, Foreign Minister Mamoru Shigemitsu, and, beside him, Army Chief of Staff Yoshijiro Umezu (who had hoped for "one last battle") will sign the Instrument of Surrender.*

INDEX

Aachen, Germany, 219, 261
Abyssinia. *See* Ethiopia
Achilles, 31
Addis Ababa, Ethiopia, 17
Aden, Gulf of, 75
Admiral Graf Spee, 31–32, 43; *ill.,* 29, 31
Admiralty Islands, 212
Africa, desert war in, 75–82, 83, 114, 139–44, 167–73 *passim. See also* specific aspects, battles, developments, events, individuals, places, units
Afrika Korps, 79–82, 95, 139–44, 162, 166, 171–73, 190, 192
Agheila. *See* El Agheila
"Aid to Finland" mission, 42–43
Airborne, The (Blitzstein), 268
Airborne troops (airborne operations), 44, 45, 83, 214, 219 (*see also* Paratroopers); first used by Germany, 44, 45
Air war (air raids), 46, 63, 177–82, 207–14 *passim,* 216, 221–22, 226, 227–28, 255–60, 268, 270, 277–79. *See also* specific air forces, aspects, battles, countries, developments, individuals, places, planes, units
Ajax, 31
Akagi, 121, 123
Alamein. *See* El Alamein, Battle of
Alam Halfa Ridge, 141
Alaska, 118
Aleutian Islands campaign, 118, 121, 122, 127, 182, 183, 212
Alexander, General Sir Harold, 141, 171, 173, 176, 207, 208, 220; *ill.,* 176, 231
Algeria, 144, 171–73
Algiers, 144, 173
Allied Supreme Council, 42–43
Alsace, 255
Altmark, 43
Americal Division (U.S.), 127
Americans. *See* United States; specific developments, events, individuals, places, units

Anami, Korechika, 279
Andalsnes, Norway, *ill.,* 60
Anschluss, 19
Anti-Comintern Pact, 14, 20
Antwerp, Belgium, 229
Anvil (Operation), 217
Anzio landings, 207, 208, 231
Arado 196 floatplane, *ill.,* 59
Archangel, U.S.S.R., 87, 130
Ardennes Forest, 29, 41, 45, 46, 47, 65, 228, 229–30, 255, 281
Ark Royal, ill., 79
Army Group A (Germnay), 45
Army Group B (Germany), 45, 47, 134, 135–39, 214, 217
Army Group C (Germany), 45
Army Group Center (Germany), 83, 87, 89, 90, 99, 139, 190, 219
Army Group Don (Germany), 137
Army Group G (Germany), 45, 214, 217
Army Group H (Germany), 261–62
Army Group North (Germany), 83, 87, 88, 90, 134, 219
Army Group North Ukraine (Germany), 219
Army Group South (Germany), 83, 87, 88, 90, 134, 190, 219–20
Army Group South Ukraine (Germany), 219–20
Arnhem, Netherlands, 219
Arnim, Colonel General Jurgen von, 171–72, 173; *ill.,* 195
Arnold, General Henry H. (Hap), 152; *ill.,* 191, 227
Athenia, 30
Atlantic, Battle of the, 129–32, 167
Atlantic Wall, 133, 214, 234; *ill.,* 234
Atomic bombings of Japan, 274, 275, 277, 279, 300, 301; *ill.,* 275
Attu, 122, 127, 182
A-20 (plane). *See* Douglas A-20 Havoc
Auchinleck, General Sir Claude, 81, 141
Australia (Australian troops), 24, 79, 80, 113, 117, 118, 119, 125, 126, 167, 183, 184, 222, 270; "coast watchers," 126; 6th Division, 79

INDEX

306

INDEX

INDEX

Typhoon, Hawker (plane), *ill.*, 245

U-boats, 12, 30, 179 (*see also*
Submarine warfare); Allied air raids
on sub pens and, 139, 177–78, 179;
U-30, 30; U-47, 30; U-81, 79
Ukraine (Ukrainians), 28, 83–84,
134, 219, 220
Umezu, Yoshijiro, 279
"Unconditional surrender" demand,
171, 266, 279–80
Union of Soviet Socialist Republics, 15,
20, 118, 132, 133–39, 167, 173,
180 (*see also* specific developments,
events, individuals, places); and
background, causes, and start of
World War II, 16, 18, 20, 24,
27–28; and capture of Berlin,
265–66; and declaration of war on
Japan, 279; German attack on
(Barbarossa Operation), 58, 82,
83–91, 114, 133–39 (*see also*
Barbarossa; Eastern Front; specific
battles, developments, individuals,
places, units); Hitler and, 15, 51, 58
(*see also under* Hitler, Adolf);
(1939), 16, 18, 20, 24, 27–28, 32;
(1940), 41, 42–44; (1941),
83–91; (1942), 133–39; (1943),
188–90; (1944), 202, 208,
210–20; (1945), 256, 260–61,
265–66, 279; Red Army of (*see*
Red Army; specific battles, units);
and Second Front, 132–33, 139,
144, 173, 187 (*see also* Second
Front); U.S. aid to, 87, 130, 133;
and war with Finland, 28, 32, 41,
42–44
United States, 13, 18, 19, 21, 91–94,
113–14 (*see also* specific
developments, events, individuals);
and aid to allies, 87, 113, 130, 333,
206; Air Force (*see* specific battles,
developments, places, planes, units;
and background, causes, and start of
World War II, 13, 19, 21; Army (*see*
specific battles, developments, events,
individuals, places, theaters of
operation, units); and invasion of
Europe, 207, 213–22, 228–30,
255–68; and isolationism, 13; and
Japanese attack on Pearl Harbor,
91–94, 113, 114 (*see also* Japan;
Pearl Harbor); Marine Corps (*see*
Marine Corps, U.S.); Navy (*see*
Navy, U.S.); (1942), 132–33, 139,
144; (1943), 167–73 *passim;*

182–87; (1944), 207ff., 228–30;
(1945), 255–80 *passim;* and *Panay*
attack, 19; and Second Front, 132
(*see also* Second Front); and
Spanish Civil War, 18
Unterseeboot, 30. *See also* U-boats
Uruguay, 31–32
Ushijima, Lieutenant Genral Mitsuru,
273, 274
Utah, ill., 93
Utah Beach, Normandy, 216

Vaagso, Norway, 132
"Val" (Japanese dive bomber), 92; *ill.*,
110
Van Kirk, Captain Theodore J., *ill.*,
274
V-E Day, 266–68
Versailles Treaty, 13, 15, 16, 21, 49, 51
Vian, Philip, 43
Vichy, France, 49, 167
Victor Emmanuel III, King (Italy),
174
Vienna, Austria, 19, 261
Volcano Islands, 187, 270
Volga River, 87, 134, 135, 137, 138
V-1 and V-2 bombs, 216, 217,
238–39
Vought Corsair (U.S. plane), *ill.*, 291,
295

Wacht am Rhein (Operation),
229–30, 255
Wainwright, Major General Jonathan
M., 117
Wake Island, 185, 222
Warsaw, Poland, 23, 27, 219; *ill.*, 26,
27, 37
Wasp, ill., 150
Wavell, General Sir Archibald, 76, 80,
81, *ill.*, 96
Wehrmacht (German Armed
Forces), 27, 140 (*see also* specific
battles, developments, events,
individuals, places, units); and Allied
invasion of Europe, 214–22 (*see
also* specific developments, places,
units); and Belgium (*see* Belgium);
and desert war (*see* Desert warfare;
North Africa; specific individuals,
places, units); and Eastern Front,
83–91, 133–34, 135–39,
189–90, 219–20, 256, 261ff. (*see
also* specific battles, places, units);
General Staff, 32, 41; High
Command, 47, 52, 80, 90; and
Holland (*see* Netherlands, the);

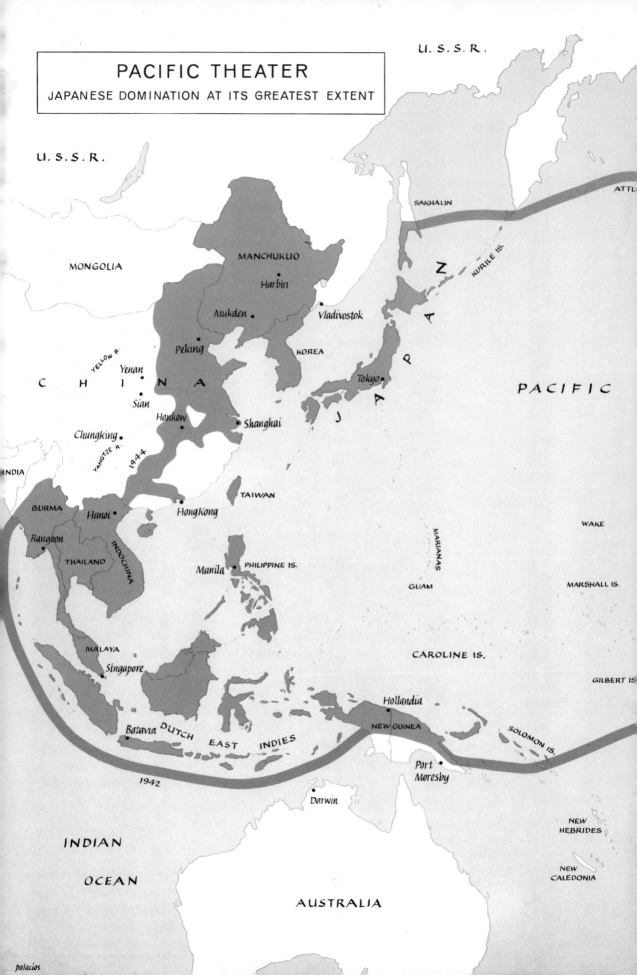

PACIFIC THEATER
JAPANESE DOMINATION AT ITS GREATEST EXTENT

U.S.S.R.

U.S.S.R.

SAKHALIN

ATTL

KURILE IS.

MONGOLIA

MANCHUKUO

Harbin

Mukden

Vladivostok

Peking

KOREA

Yenan

CHINA

Sian

Tokyo

J A P A N

Hankow

Chungking

Shanghai

YELLOW R.

YANGTZE R.

1944

PACIFIC

INDIA

TAIWAN

BURMA

Hanoi

Hong Kong

Rangoon

INDOCHINA

WAKE

THAILAND

MARIANAS

Manila

PHILIPPINE IS.

GUAM

MARSHALL IS.

MALAYA

Singapore

CAROLINE IS.

GILBERT IS

Hollandia

Batavia

DUTCH EAST INDIES

NEW GUINEA

SOLOMON IS.

1942

Port Moresby

Darwin

NEW HEBRIDES

INDIAN

NEW CALEDONIA

OCEAN

AUSTRALIA

palacios